FOOTPATHS FOR FITNESS

DORSET

Other walking titles on the county published by Countryside Books include:

PUB STROLLS IN DORSET
Anne-Marie Edwards

POCKET PUB WALKS IN DORSET
Nigel Vile

ADVENTUROUS PUB WALKS IN DORSET
Anne-Marie Edwards

PUB WALKS ALONG THE DORSET COAST PATH
Anne-Marie Edwards

WATERSIDE WALKS IN DORSET
Anne-Marie Edwards

KIDDIWALKS IN DORSET
Nigel Vile

For a full list of our walking titles, please visit our website
www.countrysidebooks.co.uk

FOOTPATHS FOR FITNESS

DORSET

Anne-Marie Edwards

COUNTRYSIDE BOOKS
NEWBURY BERKSHIRE

First published 2009

COUNTRYSIDE BOOKS
3 Catherine Road
Newbury, Berkshire

To view our complete range of books,
please visit us at
www.countrysidebooks.co.uk

ISBN 978 1 84674 137 1

Photographs by Mike Edwards
Maps by Gelder Design & Mapping

Designed by Peter Davies, Nautilus Design
Produced through MRM Associates Ltd., Reading
Printed in Thailand

CONTENTS

FOOTPATHS FOR FITNESS

GRADE 1 – EASY

GRADE 2 – MODERATE

FOOTPATHS FOR FITNESS

GRADE 3 – CHALLENGING

Introduction

'Walk a day, live a week' – this old French proverb sums up admirably the importance of walking for all of us, and the whole aim of this book. Walking is so natural and easy – you do not need any special skills, there are no rules to follow and you do not have to join expensive clubs – so it may come as a surprise to hear that it is one of the finest ways to keep fit and to lead a long and healthy life. A relaxing walk in the fresh air among interesting surroundings benefits our minds as well as our bodies. After a walk we have a sense of well-being and usually feel more able to cope with the stresses and strains of everyday living. I have found the solution to many a thorny problem whilst out on the hill.

If you are not accustomed to walking, do not set yourself too high a target at first. The walks in this book are graded so you can start with the easier, flatter walks and attempt the more challenging ones as your fitness level improves. All the walks are accompanied by simple sketch maps designed to guide you to the starting point and give an overall picture of the route, but I recommend you arm yourself with the appropriate Ordnance Survey Explorer or Outdoor Leisure map noted in the introduction to each walk. They will give you all the extra information you may need, including how to work out a grid reference.

A glance at the map shows how fortunate we are to have such a splendid network of footpaths and bridleways. These rights-of-way were shaped in the past by people in the course of their everyday lives as they walked to work, to church, to market, to the nearest inn or to visit friends. Follow in their footsteps and you will discover we still have a wealth of wildlife and a rich store of history and folklore to enjoy as well as beautiful scenery. Now, with the acceptance of 'the right to roam' we have even greater access to some of our finest countryside.

To walk in Dorset is to take a step back in time. As you follow these walks you will find rural England at its most tranquil and unchanging. Although Dorset is a small county you will enjoy an amazing variety of scenery. In this book I include some of my favourite rambles. These include walks in the Purbeck Hills with their splendid views of the Jurassic coast, the chalk downs around Cerne Abbas and the Dorsetshire Gap, and the rolling uplands of Cranborne Chase. There are visits to market towns still small enough to retain their own special character and to old world villages as charming and as varied as the scenery.

A note on what to wear and what to take with you: the Dorset countryside can be muddy even after light rainfall so it is best to wear boots or strong shoes especially on the coast path where extra grip is always needed. It is usually wise to carry a waterproof with a hood and to wear long trousers not shorts. Dorset nettles favour the sides of footpaths. On even a short walk take a drink and a sustaining snack.

I give some idea of the number of calories you may expend during your walk but as the rate we burn them at varies according to the individual this can only be a rough estimate. It is important, of course, to watch our calories, but it is much more important that we should enjoy our walks. Enjoy walking and the calories melt away by themselves! Finally, I wish you many happy hours on foot in Dorset.

Anne-Marie Edwards

Acknowledgements

As always when I write about Dorset I acknowledge my debt to Edward and Marie Swann who helped me with my research and shared with me their love of the county. My thanks also to the staff of Southampton and Totton libraries for their assistance. I am grateful to Val Lamb and all the Milton Abbas villagers who took part in devising the lovely Milton Abbas Heritage Trail which, with their permission, I have been able to include in this book. Grateful thanks also to Marion Langridge at the Kingcombe Centre who not only advised us on the best route to take through the nature reserve but revived us with tea and cakes! At Nether Compton we were made welcome by Peter and Clare Hawkins who made many helpful suggestions for our walk from Trent.

I would also like to thank Nicholas and Suzanne Battle, Paula Leigh, and all my friends at Countryside Books for making writing this book such a pleasure, our daughter Julie for her unfailing support and my friends for their encouragement. Finally my thanks as always to my husband Mike whose many duties included taking the photographs for the book. He has been my companion on every step of the way.

PUBLISHER'S NOTE

We hope that you obtain considerable enjoyment from this book; great care has been taken in its preparation. Although at the time of publication all routes followed public rights of way or permitted paths, diversion orders can be made and permissions withdrawn.

We cannot, of course, be held responsible for such diversion orders and any inaccuracies in the text which result from these or any other changes to the routes nor any damage which might result from walkers trespassing on private property. We are anxious though that all details covering the walks are kept up to date and would therefore welcome information from readers which would be relevant to future editions.

The simple sketch maps that accompany the walks in this book are based on notes made by the author whilst checking out the routes on the ground. They are designed to show you how to reach the start, to point out the main features of the overall circuit and they contain a progression of numbers that relate to the paragraphs of the text.

However, for the benefit of a proper map, we do recommend that you purchase the relevant Ordnance Survey sheet covering your walk. The Ordnance Survey maps are widely available, especially through booksellers and local newsagents.

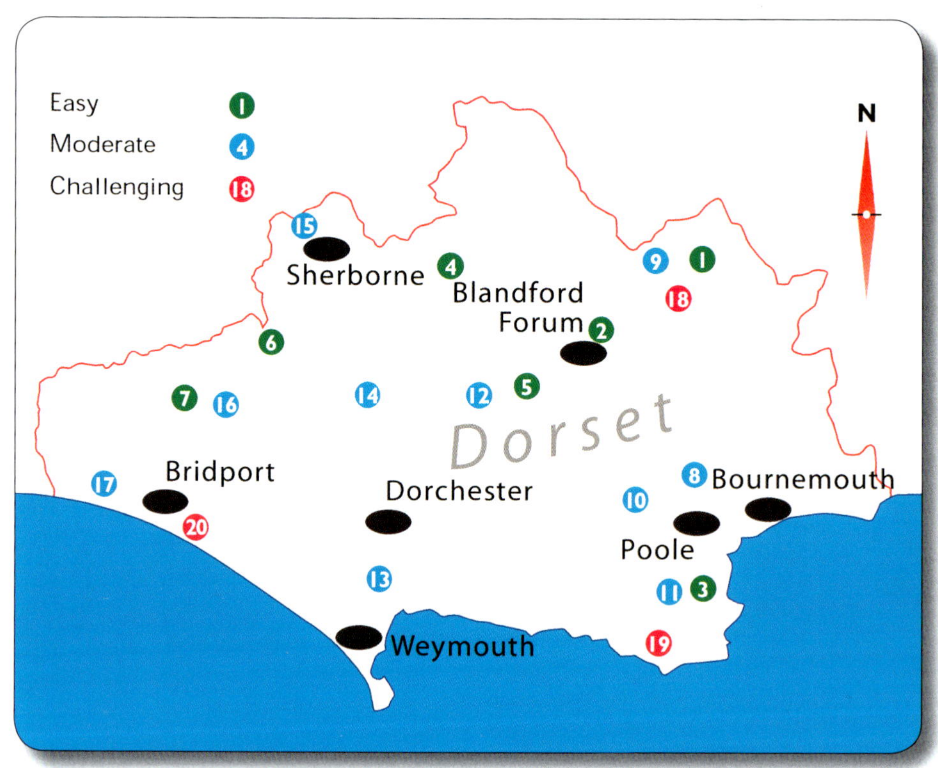

Area map showing location of the walks

1 Garston Wood

A Nature Reserve with a History

■ *The path through Garston Wood.* ■

Garston Wood is surrounded by the rolling uplands of Cranborne Chase and lies beside the Shire Rack, the ancient name for Dorset's north-west border with Wiltshire. The wood is managed by the RSPB and supports a great variety of wildlife. In spring and summer the wood is alive with birdsong. Among the many birds you may see are great spotted woodpeckers, the small mouse-like treecreepers and marsh tits. Summer migrants include blackcaps and willow warblers. The hazel and maple trees have been coppiced for many years and beneath them the ground is colourful with wild flowers. Depending on the season you will find wood anemones, primroses and bluebells and some rarer plants, including the drooping sprays of Solomon's seal, and bird's-nest and butterfly orchids. The denser oak and ash areas are home to many animals, including fallow and roe deer, badgers, foxes and dormice.

Before exploring the wood we step back in time and follow the edge of the trees along the Shire Rack. Close to this ancient border are the earth embankments of a fort that possibly dates back 3,000 years.

GRADE: 1
ESTIMATED CALORIE BURN: 300

Distance: 3 miles
Terrain: Flat woodland paths
Map: OS Explorer 118 Shaftesbury and Cranborne Chase
Starting Point: Garston Wood car park. GR 004195
How to get there: Garston Wood is about 2 miles north of Sixpenny Handley. Turn for Sixpenny Handley off the A354 along the B3081. At the approach to the village turn right into Dean Lane. At the junction keep ahead signed for Bowerchalke. The lane skirts the southern edge of Garston Wood then curves left beside the wood heading north. In a little over ½ mile look carefully for the gravelled entrance to the car park on the left – it is signed discreetly on the right of the lane.
Refreshments: The Roebuck Inn at Sixpenny Handley. A family pub with good food and real ales. Telephone: 01725 552002.

1 Return to the car park entrance and turn left to walk beside the lane for about 150 yards to a footpath sign on your left.

2 Turn left to follow the narrow path along the edge of the wood tracing the line of the **Shire Rack**. At first the path is fenced but soon opens into mixed woodlands of coppiced hazels dotted with oaks and beeches. The

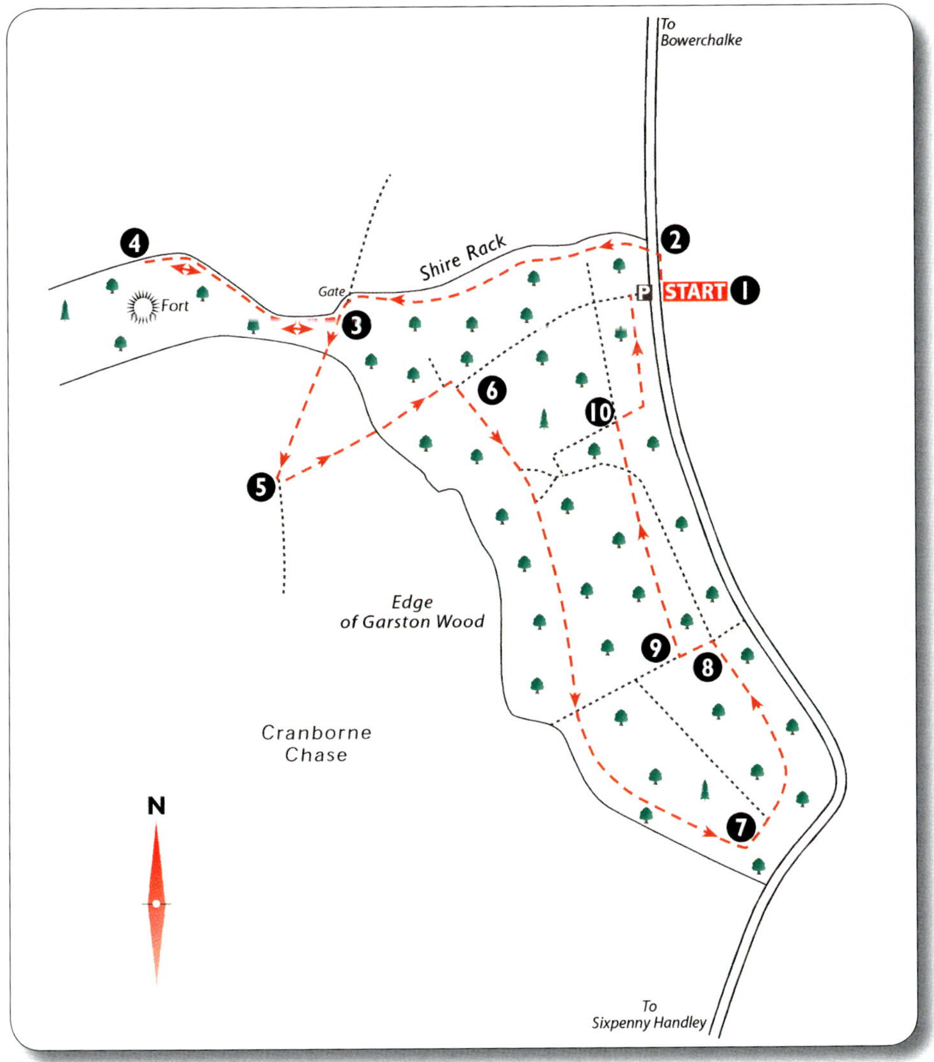

path curves left in front of a gate and after about 50 yards curves right to continue along the edge of the wood.

3 As the path curves right you will see a rather faint path leading left through a narrow neck of woodland. We return to take this path after a short detour to see the fort. So for the present continue along the edge of the wood for about 200 yards. Look through the trees on your left and you will see the

steep earth embankments of the fort. As you might expect this border country must have witnessed many battles. Not far away, at **Bokerley Dyke**, it is possible the Romanised Celts halted the advance of invading Saxon tribes into Dorset for over 100 years.

4 Retrace your steps to point 3 and turn right to follow the path through the belt of trees to emerge in open countryside with wide views over **Cranborne Chase**. Keep ahead over a field to a crosstrack.

5 Turn left and continue over the field towards the trees of **Garston Wood**. Follow the path into the wood and go through a gate. Pass a path on your left and a few yards further on you will see a wooden bench.

6 Turn right opposite the bench and follow the woodland path ahead for about ¾ mile past all paths on the left. You enter a special fenced area through a high deer gate. This area is being carefully managed by the RSPB to exclude the deer and encourage the growth of flowers such as bugle and violets favoured by a rare butterfly, the silver-washed fritillary. Leave through another high gate and continue to the southern corner of the wood from where you can see the lane ahead.

7 Turn left before the lane along the woodland path and pass a path on the left. Continue along the path as it curves along the western side of the wood heading north to a crosspath.

8 Turn left for about 150 yards to a joining path on your right.

9 Bear right to head north again. Go over a crosstrack and continue to the next crosstrack.

10 Turn right and follow the path as it curves north to bring you back to the car park.

■ *Garston Wood, managed by the RSPB.* ■

The RSPB has managed Garston Wood for wildlife and visitors since 1986. The Reserve is open at all times and dogs are permitted if they are on a lead. We are asked to keep to the defined rides and paths to avoid disturbance to wildlife. For more information about the reserve and the work of the RSPB telephone 01929 553360 or click on the website: www.rspb.org.uk.

2 Tarrant Monkton

River Valleys and Downland

■ *Tarrant Monkton Village.* ■

A few miles east of Blandford Forum the Tarrant, a sparkling chalk stream, flows south to meet the Stour past a succession of tiny villages. One of the most enchanting is Tarrant Monkton. At the turn of the 20th century the historian Sir Frederick Treves cycled through Dorset, his native county. In his book *Highways and Byways in Dorset* he described Tarrant Monkton as being 'half asleep in the sun and away from the world … a shy hamlet of thatched cottages whose walls are heavy with creepers and are hedged around by flower gardens and many orchards.' The village seems to

GRADE: 1
ESTIMATED CALORIE BURN: 250

Distance: 2 miles
Terrain: Grassy paths with one short climb
Map: Explorer 118 Shaftesbury and Cranborne Chase
Starting Point: The Langton Arms car park. The publican is happy for patrons to leave cars while walking but have a word with him first. If you do not wish to visit the pub cross the ford, continue past the pub and about 100 yards further on there is a small parking area beside the road on your right. GR 944089
How to get there: Approach the Tarrant valley via the A354 Blandford Forum – Salisbury Road. Take the turning for the Tarrant villages. Drive through Tarrant Launceston and after about ¼ mile, immediately after entering Tarrant Monkton, turn right over the ford. The road curves left to the Langton Arms which is on your right. To avoid the ford, turn left. Follow the road round as it curves right and keep straight on for about ¾ mile. At the junction turn sharp right for a few yards, then left. Turn right in front of Manor Farm and keep straight on to the Langton Arms which is on your left.
Refreshments: The Langton Arms. Telephone: 01258 830225.

have changed little with the years. From the village you cross a footbridge over the Tarrant and take a gently rising footpath with beautiful downland views before returning to your starting point close to the village inn.

1 Turn right from the pub car park entrance and continue through the village. After about 150 yards look for a footpath sign on your left.

2 Turn left to follow the sign along a narrow path which at first runs close to the side of a house. Cross the small footbridge over the **Tarrant** and follow the grassy path ahead to meet a lane. Bordered by high hedges with just the occasional house, this is **Tarrant Monkton High Street**.

3 Bear right along the High Street to a junction with a lane on the right signed for **Tarrant Monkton**.

4 Leave the lane here and turn left along a gravel track which becomes grassy and narrows to run gently uphill between high hedges and banks of wild flowers.

5 At the top of the down you meet a crosstrack. This is a perfect place to pause and enjoy the view over the rolling downs and thickly wooded valleys of **Cranborne Chase**. Turn left to walk along a wide path along the crest of the down to a crosstrack. There is a metal barrier on your right.

6 Turn left to take another pleasant grassy path downhill to meet a lane. Keep ahead down the lane to the corner of **High Street**. Keep ahead – there is a row of cottages on your left and an old well – and cross the packhorse bridge over the Tarrant. The ford is on your right. It is hard to believe that this idyllic scene was once the main route from London to Weymouth until the Great Western Turnpike (the present A354) was constructed through Tarrant Hinton in 1755.

7 At the Y-junction take the left-hand road which curves left in front of the

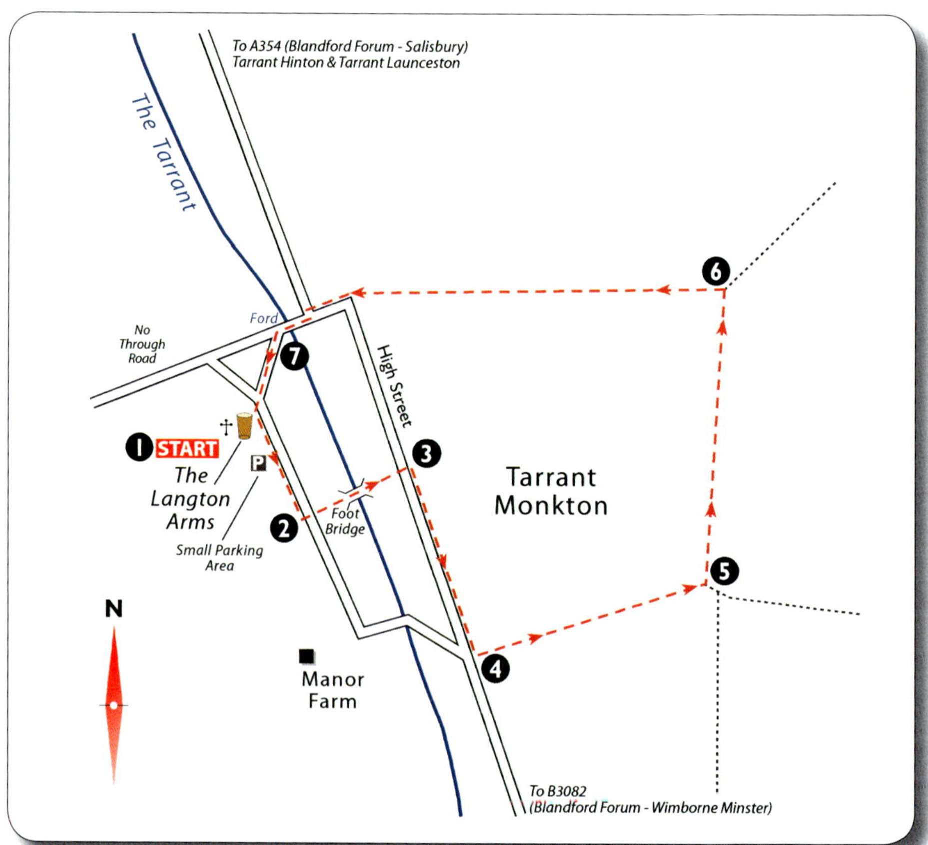

■ *Crossing the ford at Tarrant Monkton.* ■

Langton Arms to return to your parking place. Before you leave, find time to visit the nearby church which is full of interest. The tower was built in the 15th century and inside there is a bell wheel dating from 1610 that was once used for swinging the tenor bell. It was taken down in 1970 when the bells were rehung. The simple font is Norman and one of the figures in the stained-glass east window commemorates Bishop Poore who built Salisbury Cathedral. He was born a little further down the valley at Tarrant Crawford.

3 Studland & Godlingston Heath

Rolling Heathland and Sea Views

The Isle of Purbeck is famous for its spectacular scenery and wealth of wildlife. The walk begins in Studland, a small village hidden from the sea by copse woods and overlooked by a magnificent Norman church. From the village a woodland path leads to Godlingston Heath, nationally important for its rich wildlife. Rare sand lizards breed here and the birds include hobbies and nightjars. Our track over the heath rises to give wide views west over Poole Harbour and south to the chalk stacks and cliffs of the Isle of Wight before heading for the Agglestone, an enormous boulder perched precariously among the heather and gorse. We follow an attractive path through a wooded valley before rejoining our outbound route to return to Studland.

GRADE: 1
ESTIMATED CALORIE BURN: 450

Distance: 4 miles
Terrain: Moorland paths, some gentle gradients
Map: Outdoor Leisure 15 Purbeck and South Dorset
Starting Point: The National Trust car park beside the Bankes Arms. GR 038825
How to get there: From Wareham head south along the A351 towards Corfe Castle. Turn left under the railway bridge signed 'Studland 5 miles'. Drive into the village, turn right following the sign for the Manor Hotel, then right, and right again following the large brown signs for the Bankes Arms.
Refreshments: The Bankes Arms. Part of the garden overlooks the sea. Telephone: 01929 450225.

■ *On the path to Studland church.* ■

1 Turn left from the car park entrance and almost immediately turn left again following a narrow footpath signed for the church. The path leads round the north side of the church. Walk round the church to enter by the south porch. The earliest building dates from the first years of

the 11th century but it was remodelled in the 12th century by Norman craftsmen and remains a splendid example of their work with rounded arches and finely groined and vaulted roofs. Leave the church by the south porch. Don't miss the prominent gravestone to the left of the path which tells the remarkable story of Sergeant Lawrence of the 40th Regiment of Foot. He fought in all the battles of the Peninsular war and finally at Waterloo. He married a French girl and brought her home to Studland to help him run the village pub. Go through the gate and walk down the street ahead to a T-junction. There is a beautifully carved cross on the left.

2 Turn right and walk up the road to meet the B3351. Cross the road to the entrance to the village hall and turn left leaving the entrance on your right. Keep straight ahead to follow **Woodhouse Wood Walk**, taking a grassy path which leads uphill then levels to run through woods and descend to a lane.

3 Turn left up the lane. (You can take the footpath to the left of the road and after about 50 yards rejoin the lane.)

4 About 50 yards further on turn right along **Agglestone Road**. Ignore all footpath signs and keep to the gravel track as it curves left past gates on the right.

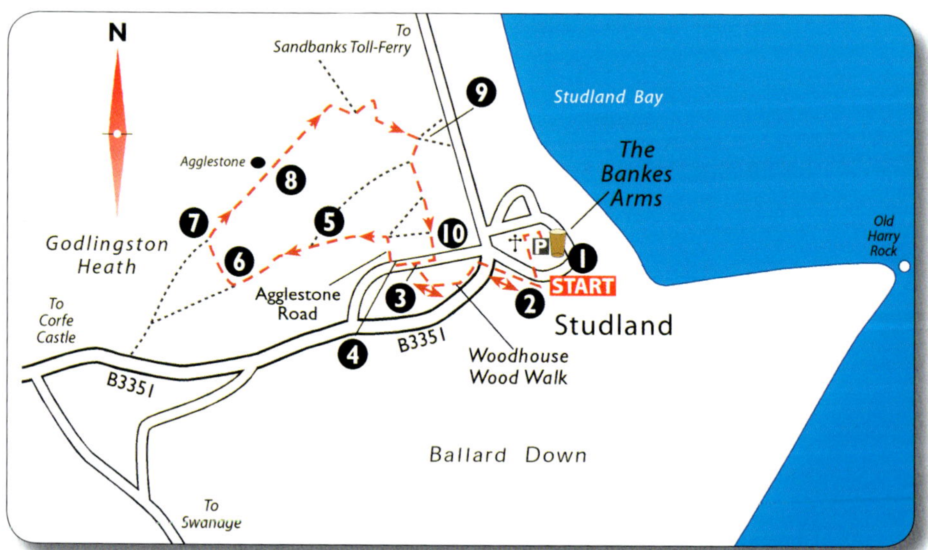

■ *Crossing the heath to the Agglestone.* ■

5 Just past the last house, ignoring a gate a little to your right, cross a stile to follow a narrow path uphill curving left to the heath. Keep straight ahead past a track on the right and continue uphill. As you near the top of the rise a track joins your way leading downhill on the right.

6 Turn right and follow the track into the valley and uphill to meet a crosstrack.

7 Bear right to follow the track along the ridge to the **Agglestone**. According to legend this huge lump of rock owes its odd situation to the Devil! He was passing time on the Isle of Wight when he decided to hurl the rock at Corfe Castle. He missed his target and it landed on Godlingston Heath instead.

8 Leave the **Agglestone** on your left, descend the steps and walk downhill. The path bears right through the trees to a small footbridge on your right. Cross the bridge and go through a gate. Keep to the main track as it curves left past a gate on the right. Continue uphill past some houses and look carefully for a track on your right marked with a blue bridleway sign.

9 Turn right through the trees for about 200 yards to a Y-junction. Take the left-hand path. At first you can take the narrow path to the left of the main track, then follow the main track past stables to meet a lane by a sign for **Heatherside Walk**.

10 Turn right along the lane for about 100 yards to **Woodhouse Wood Walk** and turn left to retrace your steps to cross the B3351. Continue retracing your earlier route leaving the village store on your left, turning left at the cross to the church, then right for the car park.

4 Sturminster Newton

A Riverside Ramble

FOOTPATHS FOR FITNESS

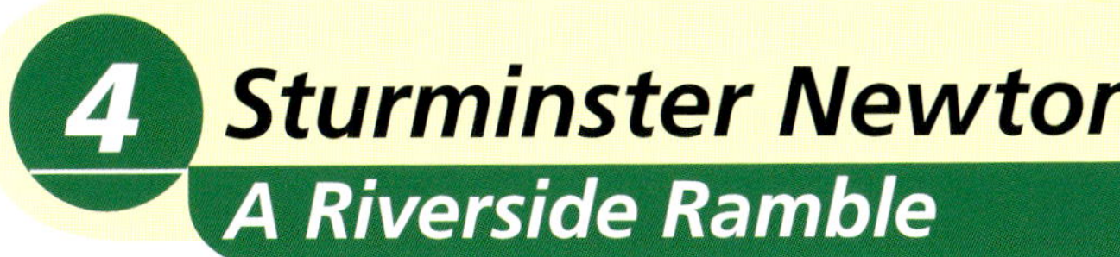

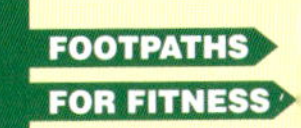

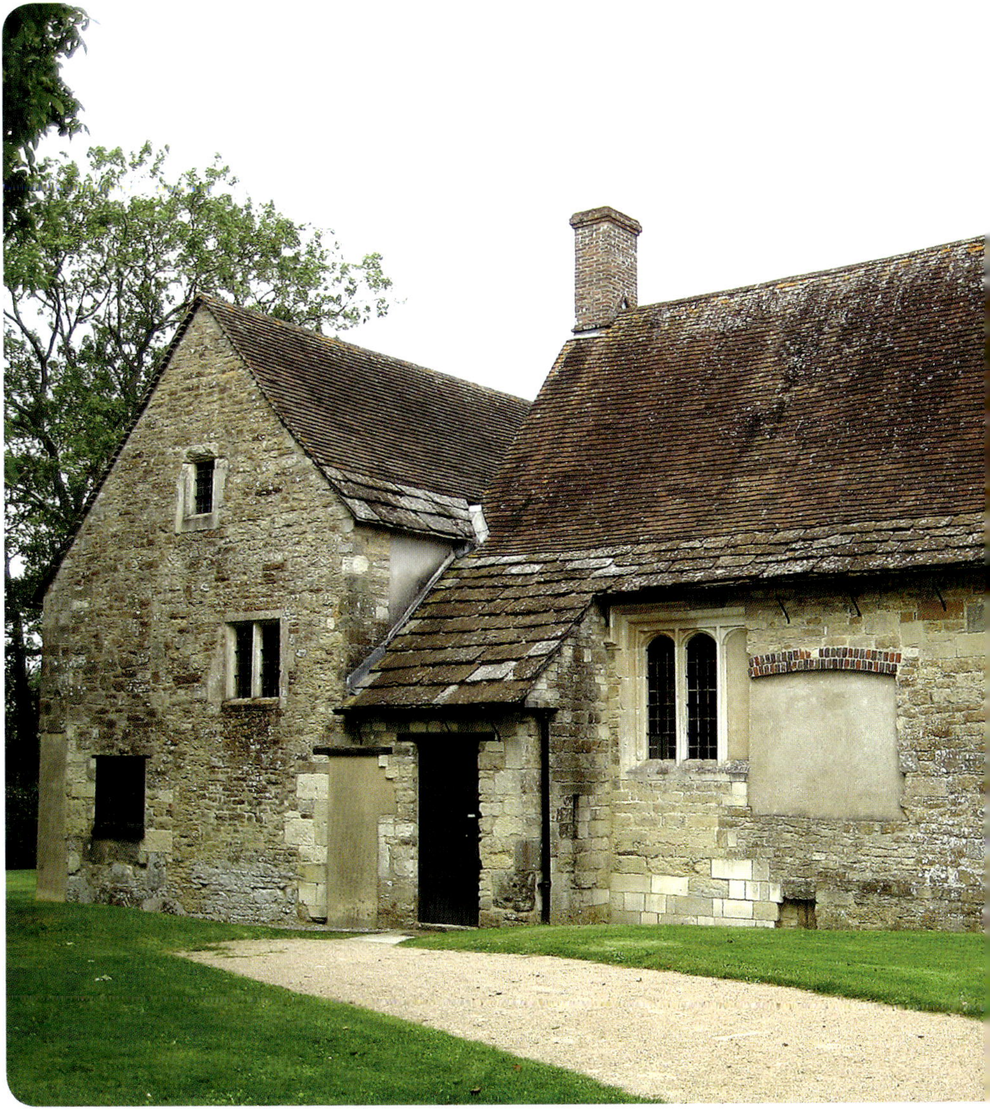

■ *Fiddleford Manor dates from the 14th century.* ■

GRADE: 1
ESTIMATED CALORIE BURN: 300

Distance: 2½ or 3 miles
Terrain: Flat meadow paths and tracks
Map: OS Explorer 129 Yeovil and Sherborne
Starting point: Sturminster Newton Station Road car park. GR 788142
How to get there: Approach Sturminster Newton via the A357. Turn for the town across the bridge, drive past the market place and follow the signs for the car park, turning right at Old Market Hill down Station Road.
Refreshments: Plenty of places to choose from in Sturminster! We recommend the friendly Poets' Corner Café on the corner opposite the car park. Telephone: 01258 473723

This gentle stroll through the meadows beside the Stour is one of my favourite walks. We start from Sturminster Newton, an old market town in the heart of the Blackmore Vale. Stur, as it is known locally, is a fascinating blend of medieval gables, coaching inns, and attractive Georgian houses and cottages. Outside the thatched market house are the octagonal steps of a cross where folk from the surrounding countryside have gathered to buy and sell since Saxon times. From the town our route follows the track of the former railway, then takes riverside paths to Fiddleford Mill. In the past this was a favourite haunt for smugglers of contraband liquor and must have seen some lively times as factory workers from Sturminster flocked to this secluded spot for a cheap drink! Close by is Fiddleford Manor which dates back to the 14th century. The magnificently timbered roofs of the hall and upper chamber are said to be the finest in Dorset and are well worth a visit. We walk back to the town along the riverside in the footsteps of Dorset's great poet, William Barnes.

1 Walk down the car park leaving the factory shop on your left. Immediately ahead you will see a wide gravelled track signed for **Fiddleford Mill** and **Manor**. This is the route of the dismantled railway which once carried passengers north across the border into Somerset and south to Poole. Continue past a gate and follow the track – now called a Trailway – for about 1 mile to a bridge.

2 Do not cross the bridge but turn right just before it and take the narrow path down to the riverside. Follow the meadow path beside the river which

■ *Crossing the meadows to Fiddleford Mill.* ■

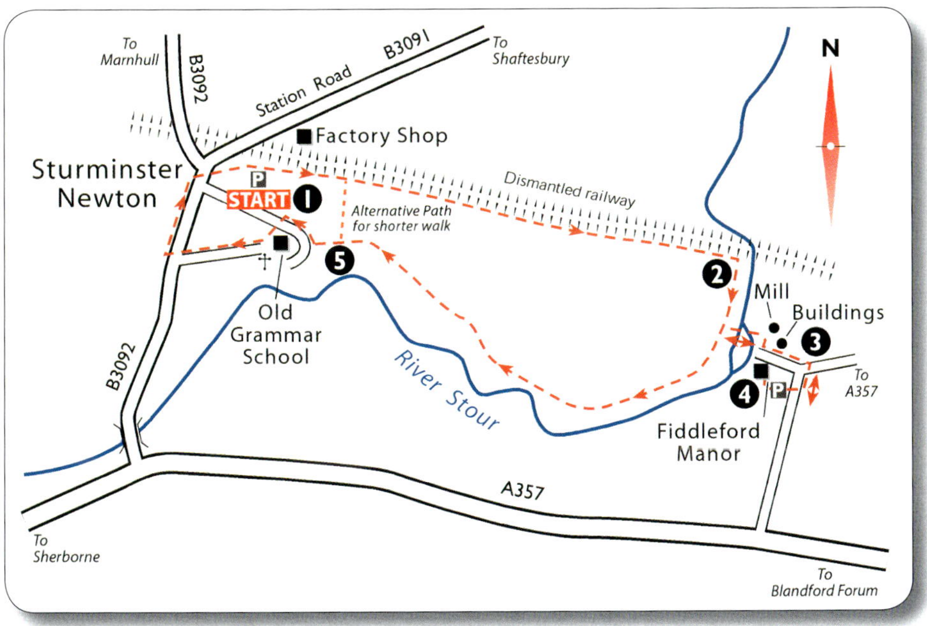

is on your left. Cross a wooden footbridge and continue along the path with views of the mill against a backdrop of wooded hillsides. Turn left to cross the bridges signed for the mill and manor. The mill is no longer in use but you will see much of its winding gear still in place. Bear right between the mill buildings and keep ahead to a lane.

3 Turn right signed for **Fiddleford Manor**. After about 100 yards turn right to cross the car park for the manor and go through a gate. A grassy path leads ahead to the entrance to the manor. You can wander at will through this fascinating building. Mind your head on some of the low archways!

4 Retrace your steps past the mill and over the bridges to the meadows. Leave your outbound route here and keep straight ahead along the meadow path. Bear left over a narrow bridge and keep ahead with the river running close beside you on the left. The river flows swiftly under the trailing willows and the still water close to the banks is overlaid with lilies, the 'clote' of William Barnes' poetry. These are the fields where he worked as a boy and recalls so happily in his poem *Rustic Childhood*. The path bears away from the river and turns left beside a hedge on the right. Go through a gate and follow the path ahead over the meadow to a gate.

5 Before the gate there is a path on the right which leads back to the railway track close to the car park. *Take this path if you prefer the shorter route*. To see more of Sturminster Newton go through the gate signed for **Penny Street**. A narrow hedged path leads you to the road. Turn right and follow the road past the high wall of the **Old Grammar School** on your left. Continue beside the wall of the school garden then turn immediately left along a narrow passage. Over the wall on your left you will see the school. The passage leads to the church – a lovely building with a barrel-vaulted roof complete with angels. Leave the church and keep ahead to the main street. Turn right past the market place to return to the car park.

5 Milton Abbas

The Heritage Trail

■ *Milton Abbey church seen from St Catherine's chapel.* ■

Milton Abbas must be the most photographed village in Dorset! Tucked firmly in a wooded valley in the downs you will find a gently curving street lined with near-identical thatched and whitewashed cottages set behind wide grassy verges. Beyond the cottages terraced gardens mount the steep hillsides. The village was planned in the 18th century by 'Capability' Brown at the request of Lord Damer, Earl of Dorchester, who, having acquired Milton Abbey, objected to the neighbouring town of Middleton and removed the inhabitants to his new village, Milton Abbas. After the dissolution of the monasteries in 1539, the abbey was largely demolished but the magnificent abbey church still stands in the idyllic setting of the Delcombe valley. Lord Damer's Gothic mansion, now a school, stands nearby. Our walk explores this unique village and its beautiful surroundings following the Milton Abbas Heritage Trail, a ramble devised by local people. The route includes a visit to St Catherine's chapel, a simple 12th-century building on a hill, half-hidden among oak and beech woods.

1 Walk up the street between the cottages passing the church and shop on your right. Pass the thatched **Hambro Arms** also on your right. Just past the old village hall picnic area you will see a bridleway sign on your left for **Haydon Plantation**. On the post is the circular **Heritage Trail** logo – a house with the date 2007.

2 Turn left uphill through the trees. The path curves left then right to a gravel track. Bear right for a few yards then left to the road at **Catherine's Well**.

3 Turn left following the sign for **St Catherine's Chapel**. When the road becomes a wide stony track continue ahead past another sign for the chapel. The track runs high through the oak and beech woods of **Pidgeon House Plantation**. Pass a house on the right and follow the track a little downhill for about 100 yards.

4 Look carefully for double iron gates on your left and a track winding half-right uphill signed for **St Catherine's Chapel**. Turn right, following the sign, past a green barrier to walk to the chapel. This little chapel in its woodland setting has a fascinating history. In the 10th century, Athelstan, first king of all England, founded the abbey in the valley below and built a chapel on this hilltop as the result of a vision. Little remains of his chapel but the present building was reconstructed in Norman times and was popular with pilgrims. On the west jamb of the south door there is a rare inscription relating to indulgences. A flight of grass-covered steps (closed) leads directly downhill from the chapel to the east side of the abbey. After various uses the chapel was restored by Everard Hambro and was rededicated.

GRADE: 1
ESTIMATED CALORIE BURN: 450

Distance: 4 miles
Terrain: Mostly flat woodland and meadow paths, one gentle climb
Map: OS Explorer 117 Cerne Abbas and Bere Regis (parts of the walk follow permissive paths)
Starting Point: Roadside parking in Milton Abbas. GR 807018
How to get there: The best approach is via the A354. Follow the signs to Milton Abbas from Milborne St Andrew or Winterborne Whitechurch. Drive downhill into the village.
Refreshments: The Hambro Arms in Milton Abbas.
Telephone: 01258 880233.

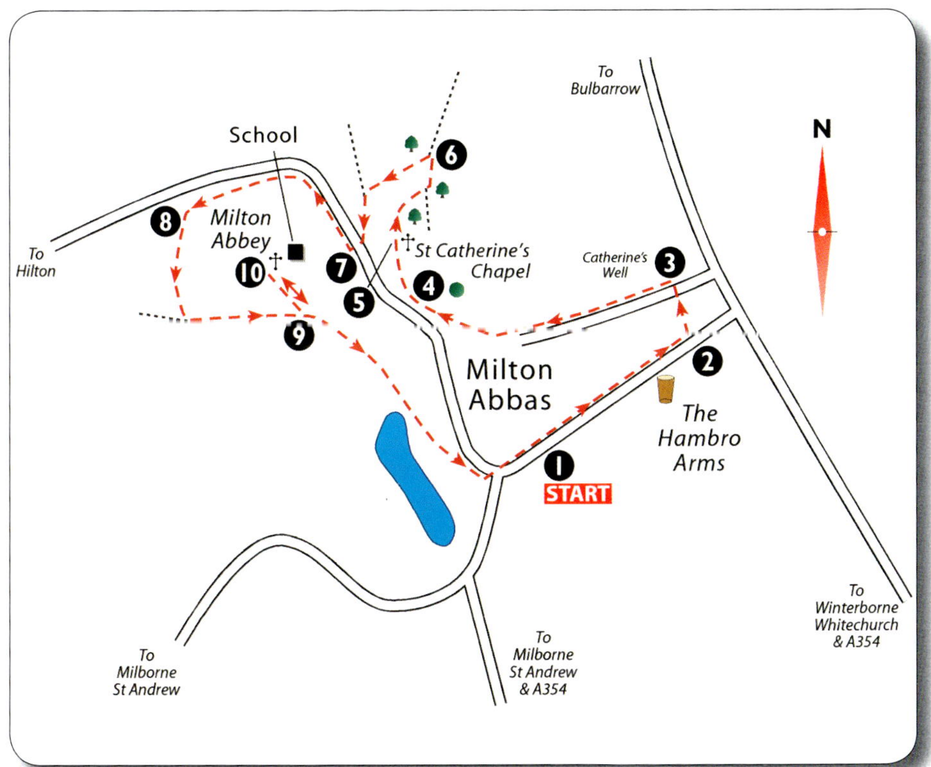

5 Follow the track round the west end of the chapel (don't miss the splendid view of the abbey) and take the path ahead. The path winds uphill to a crosspath. Bear left and continue uphill until you come to a post on the left marked with black arrows and the Heritage Trail logo.

6 Turn left steeply downhill to a crosstrack. Turn left past a barrier and follow the path, with the sloping meadows of the **Delcombe valley** on your right, to the road in front of the entrance to **Milton Abbey School**.

7 Bear right along the road for about ¼ mile as it curves round the school playing fields to a sign on your left for the abbey church marked with the Heritage Trail logo.

8 Turn left to follow the path which leads past the west front of the school and brings you past a house on the left to a lane. Turn left signed 'Milton Abbey' and continue for about ¼ mile.

9 A path on your left leads you up to the west front of this magnificent church. The abbey has many treasures including a superb 14th-century window with stained-glass by Pugin, a rare pyx-shrine – an oak tabernacle used for reserving consecrated bread – and a lovely white marble monument of Caroline, Lady Milton, who died in 1775.

10 Retrace your steps to point 9, cross the lane and take the narrow fenced path ahead which leads past the lake on your right to the road. Turn right along the pavement to return to **Milton Abbas** and your car.

■ *In the woods of Pidgeon House Plantation.* ■

6 Melbury Osmond
A Quiet Corner of Hardy's Dorset

FOOTPATHS FOR FITNESS

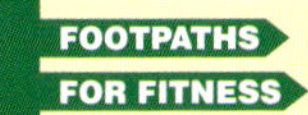

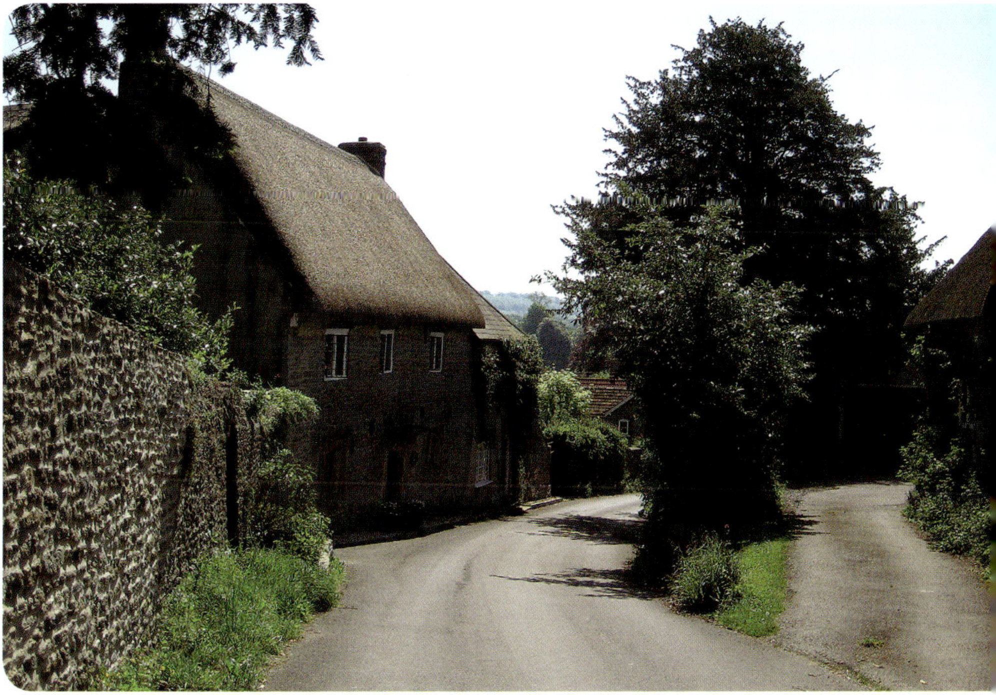

■ *Melbury Osmond.* ■

If you enjoy reading Thomas Hardy's novels, this walk will have a special appeal. The route runs through countryside he knew well and which he used as the setting for the first edition of *The Woodlanders*. We start from Melbury Osmond, a village of darkly thatched, golden stone houses where little seems to have changed since Hardy christened it 'Great Hintock'. From the village we step even further into his world to walk in the undulating parkland planted with magnificent trees which surrounds Melbury House. The park and house were bequeathed in 1523 to Henry Strangways and it is still the home of the Strangways family. In August 2000 they celebrated 500 years of residence with a huge party for the people in the neighbouring villages. Our return route follows a rather mysterious sunken track with a story to tell.

GRADE: 1
ESTIMATED CALORIE BURN: 260

Distance: 2¼ miles
Terrain: Easy flat walking. There could be a few muddy patches after heavy rain.
Map: OS Explorer 117 Cerne Abbas and Bere Regis
Starting Point: Melbury Osmond church. GR 574078
How to get there: Melbury Osmond is about ¾ mile west of the A37 Dorchester to Yeovil road. Take the turning for the village, turn left at the T-junction, then left again round to the south side of the churchyard where there is room to park.
Refreshments: None on the route but I can recommend the Acorn Inn at Evershot, 2½ miles south of Melbury Osmond.
Telephone: 01935 83228.

1 Before starting the walk find time to visit the church. Hardy's mother, Jemima, spent the early years of her life in Melbury Osmond and married Hardy's father in the church. A copy of their marriage certificate is on the wall on the left as you enter. There are two pictures of the interior of the church as it was at the time of their wedding. They stood inside the chancel beneath a much larger arch and no doubt the choir played and sang in the little wooden gallery behind them.

With your back to the church, walk down the village street. Cross the packhorse bridge over the watersplash and follow the lane ahead to the small group of houses at **Town's End**. As the lane curves right to **Clammer's Gate**, one of the entrances to **Melbury Park**, you will see a fine stone house on the left facing the gateway. This is **Monmouth Cottage**, once the home of the Swetman family, Hardy's maternal grandparents.

2 Go through **Clammer's Gate** into **Melbury Park**, 'King's Hintock Park' in Hardy's stories. An avenue of evenly-spaced trees borders the pathway to the manor. Beyond the park on the left rise the wooded slopes of **Bubb Down** and rolling away to the right are the dense woods where, in *The Woodlanders*, Grace Melbury found refuge in 'One Chimney Hut'.

3 You will see the manor ahead but before you reach it you come to a fenced turning on the left. Turn left to follow the pathway which descends over a cattle grid and crosses a stream by a cottage. Continue over another cattle grid. The pathway curves right towards **Chetnole Lodge** built in the Gothic

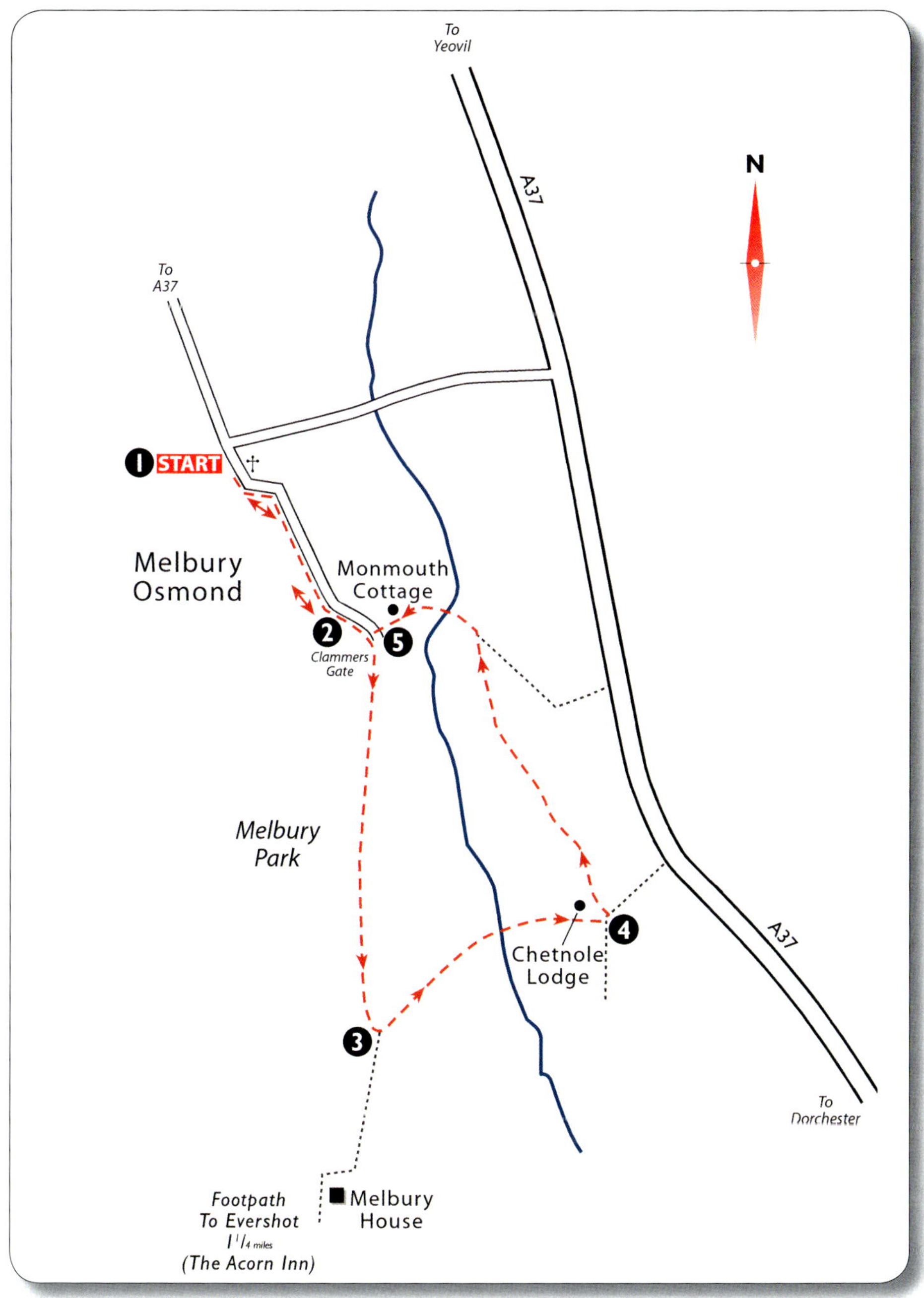
To
Yeovil
A37
N
To
A37
1 START
Melbury
Osmond
Monmouth
Cottage
2
Clammers
Gate
5
Melbury
Park
Chetnole
Lodge
4
A37
3
To
Dorchester
Footpath
To Evershot
1 1/4 miles
(The Acorn Inn)
Melbury
House

style with pointed arches and massive chimneys. Pass the lodge on your left and go over a cattle grid.

4 Cross a stream and after a few yards turn left along a wide hedged track marked with a blue arrow bridleway sign. Go through a gate and cross the open meadow ahead. Ignore the gate on your left and continue through a small wooden gate leading to a narrow sunken path heavily shaded by trees. After about 80 yards take the narrow path on the left which runs parallel to the main path to cross a wooden footbridge over a river. The path sinks deeper, runs under a tunnel and swings left to emerge in the open in front of **Monmouth Cottage**.

This is the scene of Hardy's short story *The Duke's Reappearance* which is based on a tradition which has been handed down in the Swetman family. After Monmouth was defeated at the battle of Sedgemoor most of the remnants of his army fled west. Monmouth was captured hiding in a ditch at Woodlands, not far from the New Forest. Or was he? Late one night soon after the battle, Christopher Swetman opened his door to an exhausted tall dark cavalry officer. The next day, after asking for a suit of yeoman's clothes in exchange for his own, the stranger disappeared 'through Clammer's Gate by the road that crosses King's Hintock Park to Evershead' (Hardy's name for Evershot). He left behind foreign money, an expensive Andrea Ferara sword and portraits of King Charles and his queen. Reports spread that the duke had been captured but one night the stranger returned, collected his belongings and disappeared again. Swetman always believed that his visitor was the duke and that one of his officers had been executed in his place. When I first came this way I was told that the stranger was successfully hidden from James II's soldiers in a dug-out down the path we have just followed.

5 Bear right to retrace your steps along the road and through the village to return to the church and your car.

Although Melbury House is not open there is a programme of guided walks which provides more extensive access to the park much of which is a Site of Special Scientific Interest. For information send an SAE marked 'Guided Walks' to: Ilchester Estates, the Estate office, Evershot, Dorchester, Dorset DT2 0JY.

The path past Chetnole Lodge.

7 Beaminster

Historic Town and Ancient Woodland

FOOTPATHS FOR FITNESS

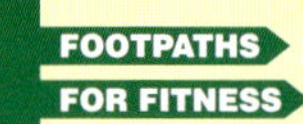

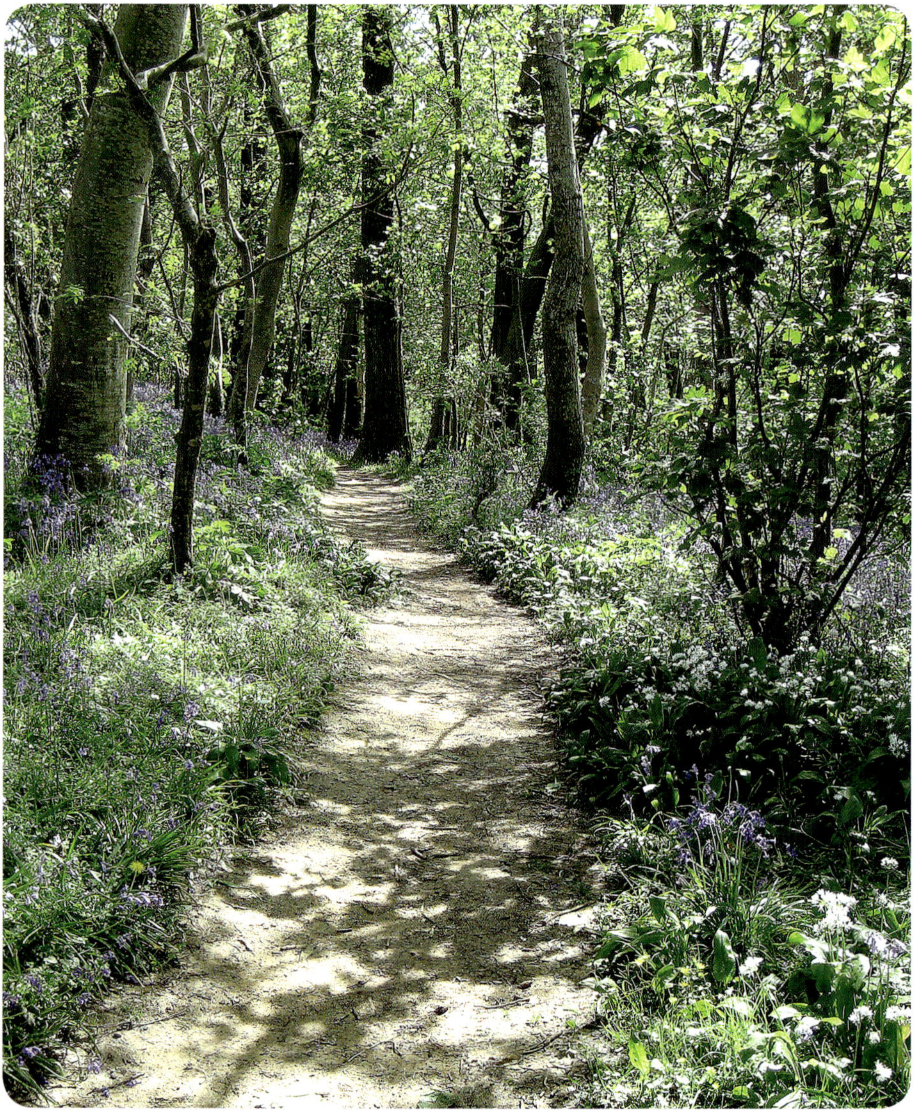

■ *The path through the wood.* ■

GRADE: 1
ESTIMATED CALORIE BURN: 250

Distance: 2¼ miles
Terrain: Flat, then one gradual climb
Map: OS Explorer 29 Lyme Regis and Bridport
Starting Point: Beaminster Yarn Barton car park signed north of the square GR 481014
How to get there: Beaminster is on the A3066 between Bridport and Crewkerne. Approaching from the west, take the B3163 from Broadwindsor. To approach from the east turn off the A356 and head for Beaminster along the B3163. Drive into the square and follow the sign for the car park.
Refreshments: Beaminster has a wealth of good places to eat including excellent pubs.

Beaminster is a small market town tucked in a hollow of the west Dorset hills. Almost all the houses are well built using the local golden stone which reflects the prosperity once derived from the wool, hemp and flax industries. As this walk is so short I hope you will have time to explore this delightful town with its splendid church, friendly old-fashioned shops and welcoming inns. From the square you follow a footpath along the valley of the river Brit. A gentle climb with wide views over the surrounding hills leads to an oak and beech wood, a quite magical place especially in early May when the trees stand in a sea of bluebells. The path runs through the wood then descends the hillside to return to Beaminster. On the way you pass St Mary's church. The 15th-century tower rises to over 100 ft among fountains of crocketed pinnacles. Figured on the west face are delicately carved scenes from the Bible.

1 From the car park return to the square, cross **North Street** and walk down **Church Street** passing the Black Cat Bistro on your right and the covered market cross – known as 'Julia', erected in 1906 by Vincent Robinson of nearby Parnham House in memory of his sister – on your left.

2 As the road curves right for the church turn left down **St Mary Well Street** then continue up the road following the sign for the **Brit Valley Way**. The asphalt becomes a wide tree-bordered track leading to a gate. Go through the gate and walk up the grassy field ahead. The trees on your left slope

down to the river in the valley. Continue through the next gate and keep ahead with a hedge on your right.

3 A few yards before your path reaches a gate directly ahead, look for a gate on your right marked with the blue arrow bridleway sign. Turn right through the gate then bear right beside a field. The path leads slightly uphill. At the end of the field keep ahead with a hedge now on your left. The path continues to rise to bring you to a gate. After the gate follow the wide track ahead.

4 Leave the track as it curves left and keep straight on through a gate with a blue bridleway sign. Now you have gained height and there are views to enjoy in all directions. The path bears right, along the hilltop, to bring you to

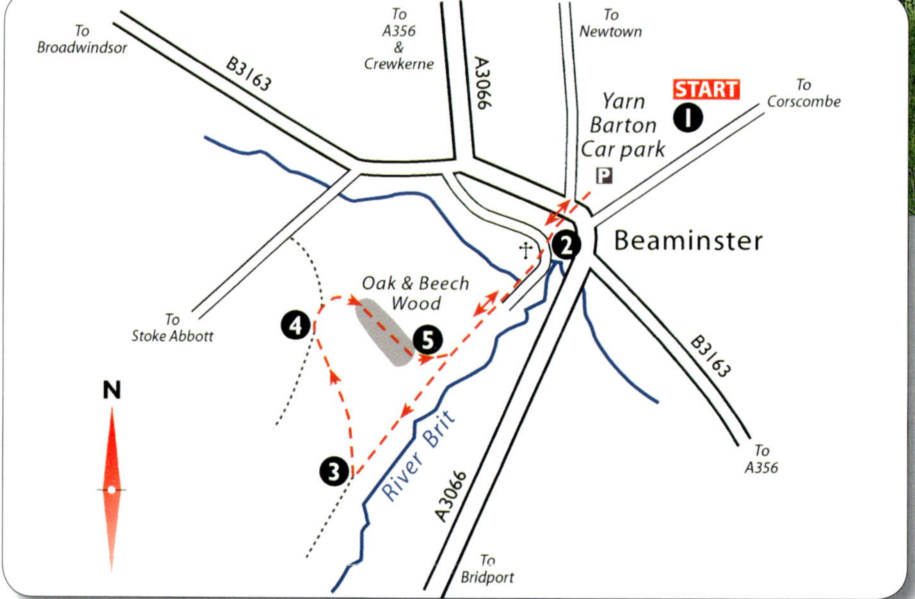

■ *Beaminster seen from the route.* ■

one of the loveliest of Dorset's woodlands. Follow the path as it weaves its way through the trees. When the path divides keep straight on (right-hand path) downhill to a stile. Cross the stile to leave the wood and emerge on the open hillside.

5 Descend the hillside, bearing slightly left, to rejoin your outbound route along the valley. Turn left to retrace your steps through a gate and along the track ahead. Turn right up **Church Street** to cross the square and return to the car park.

8 Wimborne Minster & the Stour Valley

Where Town and Country Meet

FOOTPATHS FOR FITNESS

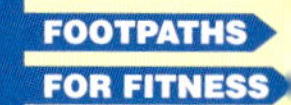

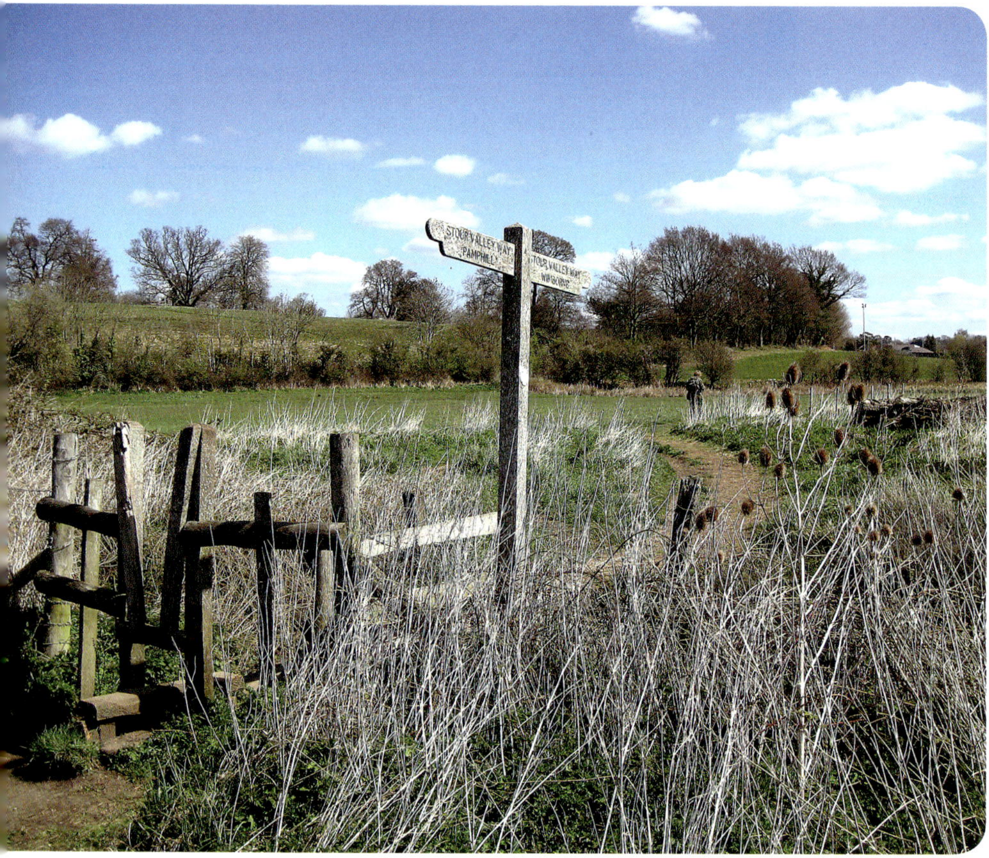

■ *Squeeze stiles on the Stour Valley Way.* ■

This is an unusual walk combining a stroll through the meadows following the Stour Valley Way with a visit to Wimborne, famous for its twin-towered minster. We start the walk at Pamphill, a small village west of the town set among wide greens, part of the Kingston Lacy estate. Lanes lead us downhill into the Stour valley to follow the riverside to Wimborne. Take your binoculars as the slow flowing river provides food and homes for a rich variety of wildlife including kingfishers, otters and water voles. We walk through the oldest part of Wimborne past the minster, cross Eastbrook Bridge which spans Wimborne's other river, the Allen, then head south beside the Poole road to cross the Stour at Canford Bridge. Attractive paths in the Stour valley lead to Eye Bridge on the course of a Roman road. Across the bridge, we retrace our steps to Pamphill.

1 With the car park on your left, follow the lane ahead past **Pamphill First School**. Endowed by Roger Gillingham, the original building dates from 1698. The school was in the higher classical centre and was flanked by eight single-room almshouses. The lane divides in front of **Pamphill Green**. Take the left-hand lane, downhill, cross the road and go over the stile.

2 Walk down the meadow towards the river and turn left to follow the riverside for about ¾ mile. When the river curves away south, the path becomes a hedged track running between allotments. The towers of **Wimborne Minster** church are directly ahead.

3 The track leaves the allotments to join a road. Keep ahead for about 50 yards, then turn left along a quiet road just before a no-through-road sign.

GRADE: 2
ESTIMATED CALORIE BURN: 700

Distance: 5 miles
Terrain: Flat, meadow paths, lanes and pavements
Map: OS Explorer 118 Shaftesbury and Cranborne Chase
Starting Point: Pamphill Green car park beside Pamphill First School. GR 993005
How to get there: From Wimborne Minster head west along the B3082 Blandford road for about a mile. Just after the sign for Pamphill Dairy turn left following the sign for Pamphill, Cowgrove and Kingston Lacy church. Pass the Dairy Farm shop and restaurant on the right and the lane to Pamphill Farm on the left and take the next left in front of the gates to the church to drive down a tree-lined avenue past a car park on the right to Pamphill Green car park on your left beside the school. If approaching from Blandford along the B3082 pass the entrance to Kingston Lacy House and, shortly, turn right for Pamphill.
Refreshments: Pamphill Dairy restaurant is near the start. Telephone: 01202 880618. Also the Vine Inn. Telephone: 01202 882259. Wimborne offers excellent opportunities for refreshments.

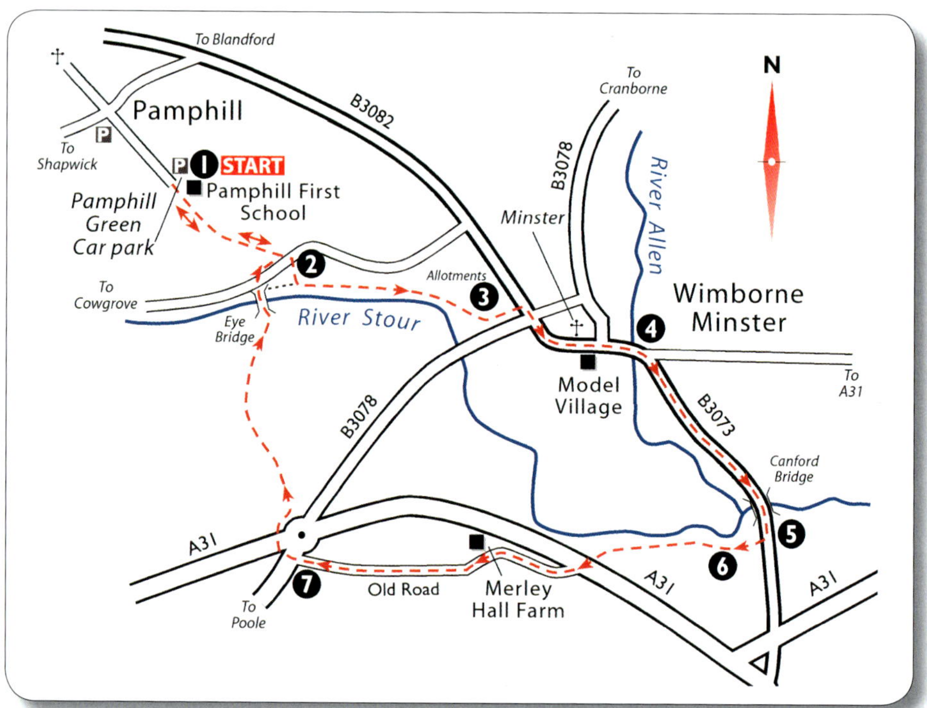

Pass the car park at the end of the road and turn right to a roundabout. Cross the roundabout (over Julian's Road) and keep ahead along **King Street** to Wimborne's minster church of St Cuthberga. She was a sister of Ine, king of the West Saxons in the early 8th century. Little of the Saxon building remains and most of the church dates from late-Norman times. Above the south vestry is the chained library established in 1686 and among the minster's many other treasures is a 17th-century astronomical clock. Continue past the entrance to the Model Town and Gardens and keep ahead across **Eastbrook Bridge** down **East Street**.

4 Turn right following the sign for Seasonal Boat Hire to the **Poole road** and continue beside the road to cross **Canford Bridge**.

5 After about 50 yards turn right along a narrow footpath signed for **Lake Gates**. When you come to a road keep straight on until the road begins to curve left.

6 Turn right along another narrow footpath marked with a no cycling sign.

There is a thick hedge at first on your left. Cross a children's playground, go through a gate and follow the footpath ahead with the Stour running through the valley on your right. When the path divides take the right-hand path downhill to follow the riverside then bear left uphill to the former road, now a pleasant track. Turn right along the track, bear left under the main road and follow the track past **Merley Hall Farm** to a road.

7 Cross the road and turn right to the roundabout on the A31. Cross the A31 to the left of the roundabout using the central refuge. Keep ahead over the grass to the fingerpost marking the **Stour Valley Way**. Continue over two stiles and follow the meadow path curving right over another stile. The path curves left to lead over a wooden footbridge and cross the meadows swinging a little right towards the river. On the hillside ahead you will see the colour-washed thatched cottages of **Little Pamphill**. The path curves more to the right past the corner of a fence to lead to the riverside and **Eye Bridge**. Cross the bridge and turn right to walk over the parking area to the road. Turn right for about 50 yards then turn left to retrace your steps uphill to **Pamphill Green** car park.

■ *The meadow path beside the Stour.* ■

9 Farnham & Chettle Down

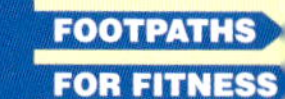

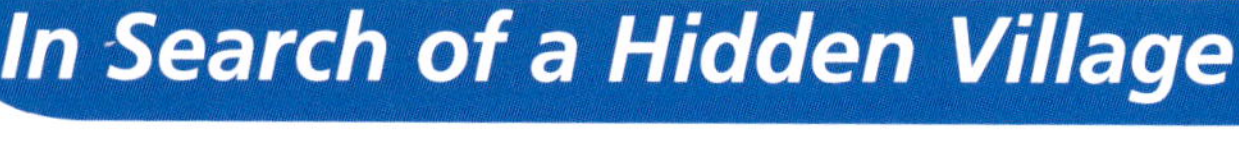

In Search of a Hidden Village

FOOTPATHS FOR FITNESS

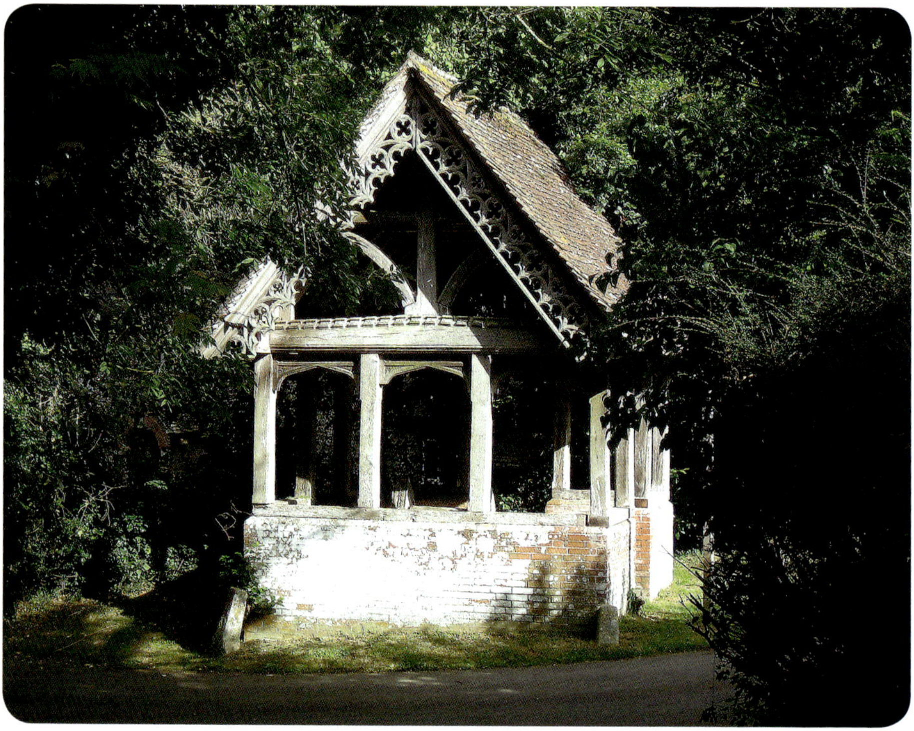

■ *The 100-year-old roofed Well House.* ■

Farnham was mentioned in the Domesday Book as 'Ferneham', meaning 'the meadow of ferns'. Set in the unspoilt countryside of Cranborne Chase the village still has an old world feel with its long street of thatched cottages, some sited end-on to the road, a brick-built Well House, and the ancient stocks beside the 17th-century Museum Inn. From the village, downland paths lead to Chettle, a tiny cluster of farms and cottages in a wooded hollow. This hidden settlement feels so remote it is easy to understand why it was once a favourite haunt of poachers and smugglers. A short detour from our route will give you a fine view of Chettle House, an elegant mansion built in the reign of Queen Anne. Meadow paths and lanes lead back to Farnham.

GRADE: 2
ESTIMATED CALORIE BURN: 500

Distance: 4 miles
Terrain: Mostly flat downland paths
Map: OS Explorer 118 Shaftesbury and Cranborne Chase
Starting Point: Parking area opposite the Museum Inn on the right in front of the children's playground. GR 958151
How to get there: Farnham is best approached from the south via the A354 Blandford-Salisbury road. Turn for the village, following the sign, at Thickthorn Cross. Take the first turning on the left. The road curves right to a junction. Turn right to drive downhill into the village. You will see the Museum Inn on your left just before a T-junction.
Refreshments: The Museum Inn in Farnham, telephone: 01725 516261, or buy a snack at the little shop in Chettle half-way round the walk.

1. With the playground and telephone box on your left walk up the road signed for Chettle. You pass the lane to the church on your right and if you look over the grass you will see the 100-year-old roofed **Well House**. Continue uphill for about 50 yards.

2. Turn left up the bank following the footpath sign and cross a stile. Keep ahead beside a field with a hedge on the left. Cross the next stile and continue ahead with a fence on your left. Go over another stile and keep ahead with a hedge on your right until the hedge ceases and you are faced with an open field.

3. Walk straight on over the field making for a small electrical installation you will see ahead, to a gap in the hedge crossed by a narrow barrier. Negotiate the barrier to descend two steps to a lane. (You may prefer to go through the gate a few yards away.)

4. Turn right along the lane for about 100 yards then turn left following the bridleway sign and the green sign for the **Ramblers' Jubilee trail**. The path leads beside a field with a hedge on the right. Go through a gate to a lane.

5. Bear right for a few yards then turn left following a bridleway sign. Continue beside a field with a hedge on your left. Go through a gate and walk beside

the next field with a hedge still on your left. The path dips gently downhill through a gate then rises a little to run between hedges. Now an attractive green track leads down into the **Chettle valley** to meet a crossing lane in Chettle village.

6 Our route turns right here but if you would like to see Chettle House you can make a short detour by turning left past Chettle shop and about 100 yards further on turning right signed for **Chettle House**. Continue uphill past the church and the drive to Chettle House into the caravan field. Turn immediately left through the trees for a fine view of the house. Part of Chettle House is open to the public on the first Sunday of each month from Easter to September from 11 am to 5 pm. For Bank Holiday openings and

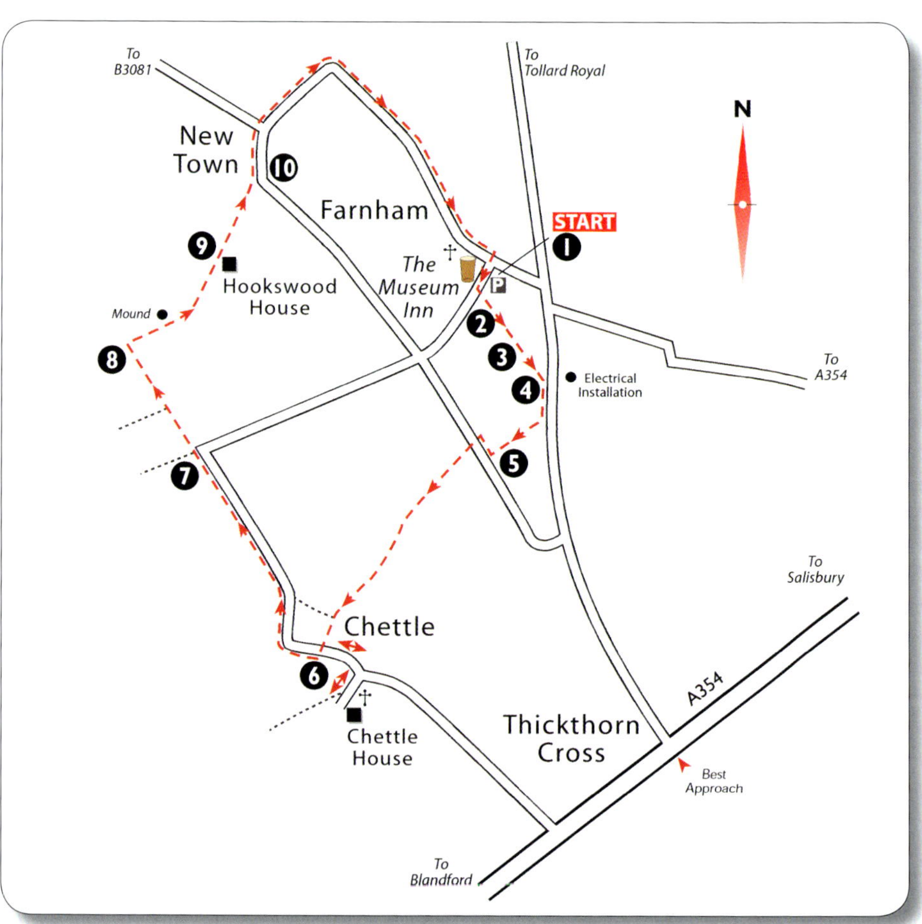

■ *Cranborne Chase from the Farnham Downs .* ■

details of special events telephone 01258 830858. Retrace your steps to point 6. Having turned right (*straight on if you made the detour*) follow the lane for about ½ mile as it leaves the village and curves right uphill.

7 When the lane turns right keep straight ahead following the bridleway sign past a gate along a tree-shaded track which runs a little downhill to open fields. Keep ahead between the fields until you reach a hedge with a wire fence.

8 Turn right beside the field with the hedge and fence on your left towards a prominent mound. Skirt the mound and at the far corner of the field bear left through the gap in the hedge and follow the field path downhill with a hedge on your right, passing **Hookswood House** on your right, to an iron gate and bridleway sign.

9 Turn right through the gate then left up the tarmac lane to meet a road at **New Town**.

10 Turn left up the road for about 200 yards to a junction – watch for traffic. At the junction bear right to follow the lane running downhill and curving right to lead you through **Farnham** back to your car.

10 Morden & Woolsbarrow Hill Fort

Dorset in Miniature

■ *A country scene near Morden.* ■

Morden is a scattered community of several small hamlets set in a landscape of low grassy hills and meandering streams. The valleys are dotted with woods that are thickly carpeted with bluebells in May. These quiet woodlands are home to many wild creatures including roe deer. Our walk begins from a large parking area beside the B3075 near the Cock and Bottle pub and explores the gentle countryside before entering a completely different world. Undulating paths lead through the heather and gorse of Wareham Forest to Woolsbarrow Iron Age hill fort which rises impressively in the centre of a clearing giving far-reaching views south to the Purbeck Hills and west over a wide expanse of rolling heathland. We return through the ancient oak woods of Morden Park then take a quiet lane back to our starting point.

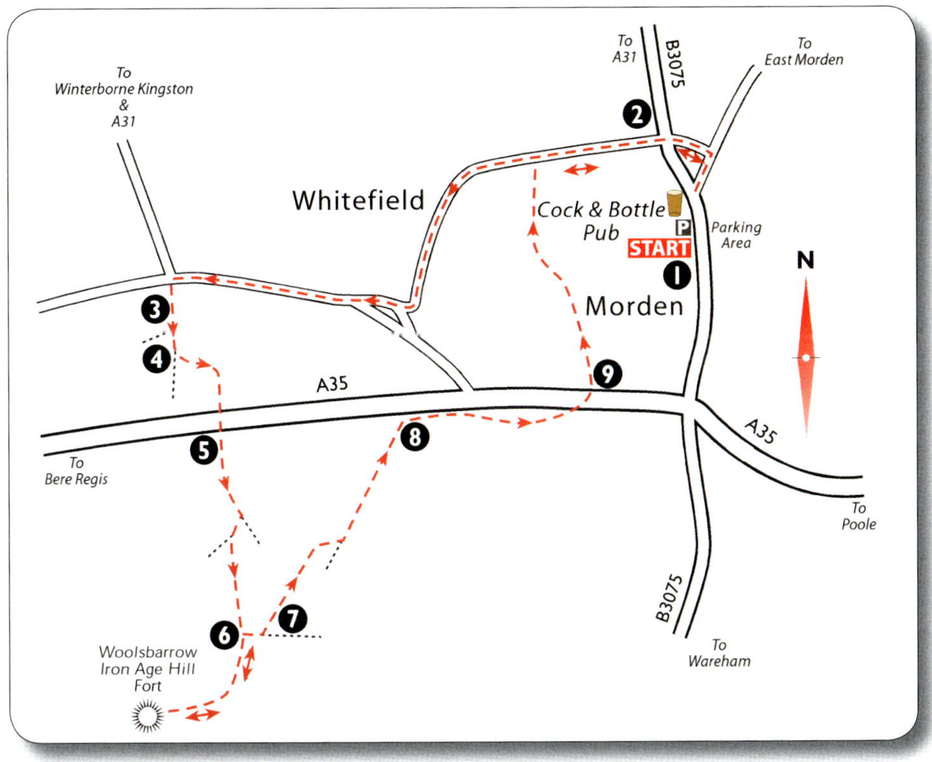

GRADE: 2
ESTIMATED CALORIE BURN: 750

Distance: 5 miles
Terrain: Quiet lanes, woodland and moorland paths
Map: OS Explorer 118 Shaftesbury and Cranborne Chase
Starting point: Parking area in Morden beside the road near the Cock and Bottle pub. GR 914946
How to get there: Morden is about 6 miles west of Poole. The B3075 links the A31 with the A35. Approaching from the A31 turn for Morden by the World's End pub. Follow the B3075 for about 3 miles to the parking area on the right just past the Cock and Bottle pub. Approaching from the A35 follow the sign for Morden for about ¾ mile to the parking area.
Refreshments: The Cock and Bottle pub, a traditional thatched inn. Telephone: 01929 459238.

1 Before starting the walk don't miss the map of **Morden** on the left of the entrance to the pub car park. It's a mine of historical information. To avoid a short stretch of the B3075, turn right up the lane opposite the pub following the sign for **East Morden**. Take the first lane on the left which bears left to meet the B3075.

2 Cross the road and follow the lane ahead signed for **West Morden**. The lane heads west through attractive countryside passing the former Wesleyan chapel, dated 1873. After about ¾ mile you come to **Whitefield**, a small group of thatched houses. The spring close to Whitefield Farmhouse is the source of the river Sherford which flows south-east to Poole Harbour. Continue along the lane, which swings left then right to cross the **Sherford**. After about a mile look for a signpost on the right. A lane on the right is signed for **Winterborne Kingston**.

Looking west from the top of Woolsbarrow Hill Fort.

3 Leave the lane and turn left along a bridleway known as **Methodist Lane** where there was a chapel a few years ago. When the main track curves right keep straight on.

4 At this point a private track leads straight ahead uphill. Our way swings left then right, past a deep-thatched house, to the A35.

5 Cross the road and follow the woodland track ahead. After about 100 yards you come to a stream. Bear a little left to cross a bridge to a fork. Navigate carefully at this point! Do not follow the track immediately ahead but take the right-hand path. Follow this for about 50 yards until it begins to curve right. Leave the track and take the narrow sunken path straight ahead leading slightly uphill through the woods. The path winds through the trees then becomes a wide way crossing open heathland. You will see the embankments of **Woolsbarrow** hill fort rising steeply ahead. Walk towards the fort to a fork.

6 The track on the left is our return route but make a short detour here to climb the fort. Keep straight on for about 50 yards to the foot of the embankments. Look for a narrow path on the right and climb this to the crossing track on the top of **Woolsbarrow**. Looking south it is possible to see Corfe Castle in its dip in the Purbeck Hills. Turn right to cross the fort to enjoy the view looking west. Retrace your steps down the side of the fort bearing left to point 6. Turn right and follow the track heading east for about 100 yards.

7 Take the first track on the left which leads over the heath to a crosstrack. Turn left to walk through the woods of **Morden Park** to meet a tarmac lane which leads to the A35.

8 Just before the road turn right along a path running parallel with the road but sheltered from it by a thick hedge. The path winds a short way from the road to lead through trees and cross a bridge over a stream. After about ¾ mile the path curves left to meet the A35.

9 Cross straight over and take the track ahead signed for **Morden** past a gate. A grassy way bordered by woods leads a little uphill for almost a mile to meet the lane we followed outbound. Turn right to retrace your steps, crossing the B3075 to take the lane ahead. Turn right at the T-junction to return to the **Cock and Bottle** and the parking area.

11 Nine Barrow Down

History & Views in the Purbeck Hills

FOOTPATHS FOR FITNESS

■ *The terraced path to Nine Barrow Down.* ■

This is a magnificent ridge walk in the heart of the Purbeck Hills. Nine Barrow Down runs east from Corfe Castle to the sea just north of Swanage. From the path along the crest of the down there are spectacular views north over the moors, Poole Harbour which is dotted with islands, Studland Bay and the inland sea. Looking south the scene could not be more different! The ridge slopes down to a green valley with farms shaded by woods and small thickly-hedged fields. Beyond the valley, over the jagged

GRADE: 2
ESTIMATED CALORIE BURN: 750

Distance: 5½ miles
Terrain: High downland paths, some gently climbing
Map: OS Outdoor Leisure 15 Purbeck and South Dorset
Starting Point: Large lay-by beside the Ulwell road opposite the Ulwell Cottage Caravan Park. GR 022809
How to get there: Ulwell is best approached from the north via the A351 Wareham-Swanage road. Before entering Corfe Castle turn left along the B3351 in the direction of Studland. After about 5 miles look for a road on the right signed 'Swanage 2½'. Turn right down the road to a large lay-by on the left marked with a large 'Welcome to Swanage' sign.
Refreshments: Ulwell Cottage Caravan Park includes the Village Inn which is open to all. The entrance to the Park is opposite the lay-by. Telephone: 01929 422823.

outline of the coastal hills, there is the glimmer of the sea. We start the walk from Ulwell, a village close to the southern slope of the down and follow an ancient pathway along the ridge for about 3 miles. Nine Barrow Down is famous for its prehistoric burial mounds, the oldest of which could date back some 5,000 years. Our return route follows a path along the foot of the down winding through woods and over open grassland colourful with wild flowers.

1 Cross the road in front of the lay-by and turn right along the pavement. When the pavement ceases continue for a few yards to a stile and footpath sign for **Nine Barrow Down** on your left.

2 Turn left over the stile and follow a narrow path which is parallel with the road at first then bears a little right to a gate into the caravan park and a marker stone indicating the path to **Nine Barrow Down** on your right. Turn right to take this attractive grassy path which runs across the side of **Round Down** to bring you to a stony track.

3 Turn right up the track, following the sign for **Corfe Castle**. After only a few yards you meet a crosspath. Turn left to follow the ridge path uphill. As you climb the valley opens on your right. The burial mounds in the valley are known as the Giant's Grave and the Giant's Trencher.

4 Pass the underhill path on your left and continue uphill to **Nine Barrow Down**. The views become even more breathtaking as you gain height. After going through a gate the path curves a little right, then, as you near the top of the hillside, it swings left to follow the ridge heading west. Soon you will see, beyond the curve of the down, the grey outlines of Corfe Castle guarding the pass in the Purbeck Hills. Continue through another gate past a path on the left for **Knitson**.

5 The next gate leads you to **Ailwood Down**, owned by the National Trust. On your right you will see a prominent cluster of Bronze Age burial mounds. Although the mounds have possibly crowned the ridge for over 3000 years the largest is still over 10 ft in height. They are grouped around the even older Long Barrow. Go through a gate to leave **Ailwood Down** and continue ahead for about ½ mile.

6 You will have passed several marker stones on the route but look carefully for a stone marked 'Corfe 1¼ ,Studland Rd ½ , Rempstone 1.' The other side of the stone is marked Ulwell 2½ , Woolgarston ½'. This is our way. Turn left to descend the hillside along a terraced path.

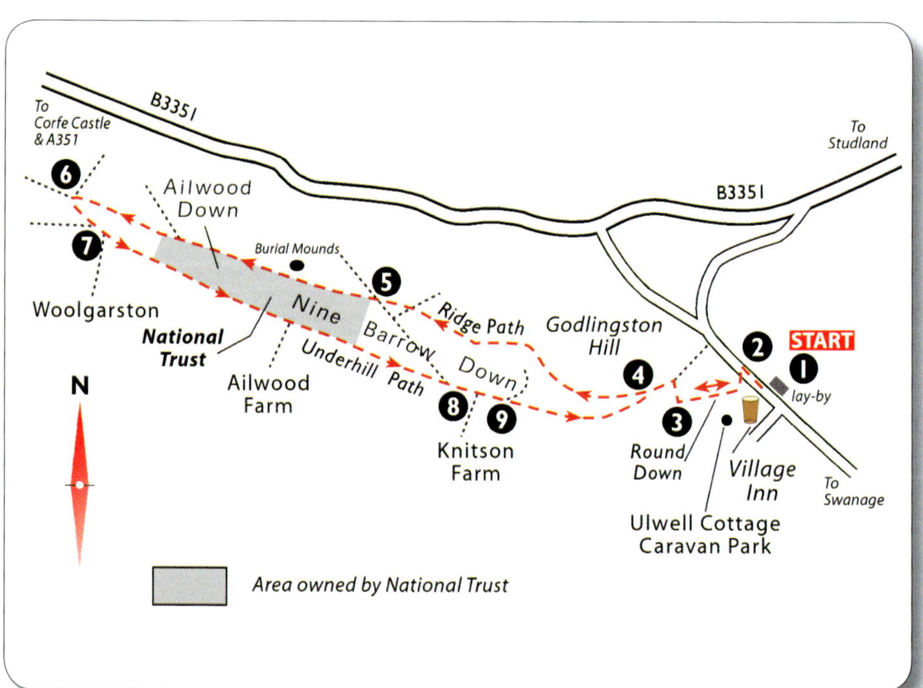

■ *Round Down near Ulwell.* ■

7 Navigate carefully here! The track divides a few yards before a gate. Do not follow the obvious track leading downhill through the gate but take the narrow left-hand path uphill. (There is a marker stone for Ulwell but it is half submerged.) Follow the narrow path along the hillside. Through a gate the undulating path tunnels through the trees and bushes then crosses more open areas, purple with foxgloves in late summer.

8 When the path divides again continue along the path ahead (the left-hand path). This leads uphill. The other path runs down to **Knitson Farm**.

9 At this point the path you are following swings left sharply uphill. Do not follow it but keep straight ahead along a grassy path through a gate. Follow the path to join our outbound route at point 4. Retrace your steps downhill heading for **Ulwell**, turning right down the stony track to rejoin the path across Round Down and return to the gate into the caravan park. Turn left to follow the path to the road and return to the lay-by and your car.

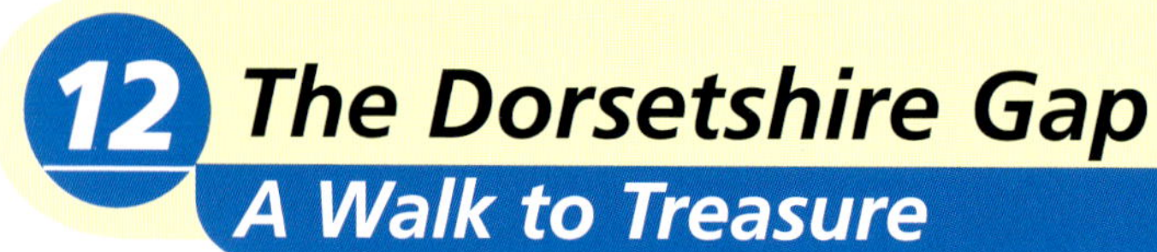

12 The Dorsetshire Gap

A Walk to Treasure

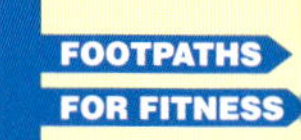

■ *View of Nettlecombe Tout from the Wessex Ridgeway.* ■

This walk takes you to one of the most thrilling places in the county, the Dorsetshire Gap. For thousands of years generations of travellers have made their way through this narrow cleft cutting through the downs north of Dorchester linking the chalk river valleys with the Blackmore Vale. Today you can walk in their footsteps and find few changes. The steep slopes of Nettlecombe Tout rise west of the pass. In summer the high ridge of downland to the east is brilliant with wild flowers. From the ridge there are magnificent views north over the Blackmore Vale and south over the downs to the coastal hills. There is more to enjoy as the route includes part of the historic Wessex Ridgeway and the site of an abandoned medieval village.

1 Turn right from the parking area beside the village hall to walk downhill past the pottery and cross a small stream, the **Devil's Brook**. Locally it is known as **Mash Water** as it was once the drain from the brewery. Continue uphill.

2 As you approach the first houses in **Melcombe Bingham**, turn right opposite the village sign following the direction for **Melcombe Park Farm**. This is **Cothayes Drove**. Follow the lane as it climbs gently uphill for about a mile passing **Cothayes Farm** and a bridleway sign on the left. Continue past **Breach Wood** on your right.

3 The lane curves left in front of a barn. At this point the lane follows part of the **Wessex Ridgeway** running between wide grass verges shaded by oak trees. After about 100 yards look for a set of flat boards to the left of the lane. They are finely carved with a poem celebrating Dorset's countryside.

GRADE: 2
ESTIMATED CALORIE BURN: 550

Distance: 5 miles
Terrain: Downland paths and tracks, easy walking
Map: OS Explorer 117 Cerne Abbas and Bere Regis
Starting Point: Beside the village hall in Lower Ansty GR 765032
How to get there: The walk starts from Lower Ansty, a small downland village. The best approach is via the A354 Blandford Forum – Dorchester road. Turn off the A354 in Milborne St Andrew following the sign for Ansty and Milton Abbas. There is also a brown sign for the Fox Inn at Ansty. After about 2 miles turn left for Ansty. After about 4 miles turn left again at Ansty Cross following a sign for Melcombe Bingham. In about ½ mile pass the Fox Inn on your left and continue a little further to the stone-built village hall which is on your right. The hall stands on a grassy mound with a tree and a seat.
Refreshments: The Fox Inn. This 200-year-old house was the family home of Charles Hall who founded the well-known brewery here in 1777. Telephone: 01258 880328.

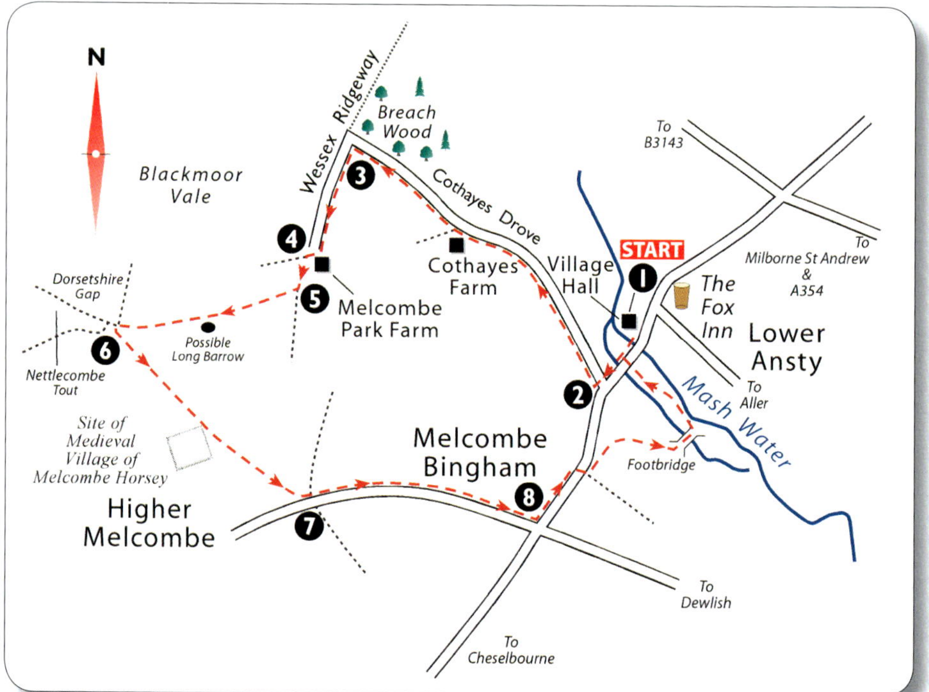

4 Opposite **Melcombe Park Farm** bear right for a few yards following the sign 'Dorset Gap'. Bear left up the farmyard passing the farm buildings on the right and go through the furthest right of three gates signed 'Dorset Gap'.

5 Follow the direction of the sign along the foot of a rising meadow with woods on your right. Go through two gates and keep ahead along the crest of a high ridge towards the wooded slopes of **Nettlecombe Tout**. On the left you pass what I believe to be a Neolithic Long Barrow where people buried their dead over 4,000 years ago. The ground drops steeply to a gate. Through the gate you arrive at the meeting of several ways at the highest point of the **Dorsetshire Gap**. Don't forget to sign the visitors' book in the box on your right.

6 Turn left to follow the old sunken track leading to the Gap following the sign for **Higher Melcombe**. It plunges steeply downhill and brings you to a gate. Through the gate our path leads beside a field with a hedge on the right. Go through two gates and continue beside a meadow with the

hedge still on your right. Beyond the hedge you will see ridges and hollows, the remains of the medieval village of **Melcombe Horsey**.

7 Go through a gate to a narrow lane and turn left along the lane to a road.

8 Turn left for **Ansty**. After about 200 yards you come to **Melcombe Bingham**. Look for a footpath sign on the right signed for **Mash Water**. Turn right between the houses to go through a gate. Ignore the obvious path leading ahead and turn immediately left with a wall and hedges close on your left. Follow the path as it curves round the edge of a field. After about ¼ mile go through a gate and follow the narrow path downhill to a small footbridge on your left. Cross the bridge and keep ahead with a hedge and Mash Water on your right. After about 80 yards cross a stile on your right and continue with **Mash Water** on your right. The path swings left up a bank then curves right to bring you to a stile and the **Ansty road**. Turn right to walk the few yards back to the village hall and your car.

■ *The site of the medieval village of Melcombe Horsey.* ■

13 Upwey & Ridgeway Hill

FOOTPATHS FOR FITNESS

Attractive Village & Splendid Views

The Wishing Well gardens at Upwey.

Upwey, where we start this walk, is a small grey-stone village in a wooded cleft in the downs north of Weymouth. As its name suggests, the village lies at the source of the river Wey. Here the river rises from two springs which bubble beneath a deep well which has become famous as a 'wishing well'. To visit, call in at the Wishing Well Café. The well is flanked by stone arches and has pride of place in the café's beautiful water garden. Don't forget to toss a coin in the well and wish! From the village we climb Ridgeway Hill following the track of a Roman road. A short stroll along the Ridgeway gives far-reaching views before we descend a valley in the downs and take a streamside path back to the village.

GRADE: 2
ESTIMATED CALORIE BURN: 400

Distance: 3½ miles
Terrain: Mostly meadow paths and tracks. One fairly steep climb.
Map: OS Outdoor Leisure 15 Purbeck and South Dorset
Starting Point: Church Street, Upwey GR 662851
How to get there: The best approach is via the A354 Dorchester – Weymouth road. Turn for Upwey (there is also a large sign for the Old Ship Inn) drive through Elwell and turn right into Church Street at the T-junction. Park beside the road just before the Wishing Well Café. If there is no room continue past the café, straight on at the junction, to the church (there is a small car park on the left but on Sundays this is reserved for churchgoers) and start the walk at point 2.
Refreshments: I recommend the Wishing Well Café (licensed) for excellent lunches and teas and friendly service. Telephone: 01305 814470. Also the Old Ship Inn. Telephone 01305 812522.

1 Walk up **Church Street** past the **Wishing Well Café** on your left.

2 At the junction follow the main road as it curves right up **Goulds Hill** for about 50 yards to a footpath sign on the right.

3 Turn right following the sign and continue past houses and along a grassy path running across the top of a garden to a stone stile. Climb the stile and take the narrow path ahead with a fence close on the right. Climb another stone stile to a meadow and keep ahead with a wall at first on your right. Steps take you over the next stile and now a grassy hedged path leads ahead. Already, looking south, there are wide views over Weymouth. Go through a small wooden gate to cross the grass and go through another small gate to a stony track. Continue up the track through another gate. A few yards further on you come to a gate and a footpath sign on your left at the foot of a wide grassy path.

4 Turn left to follow the path uphill with a tall hedge on your right and a wire fence on your left.

5 The path curves a little right to meet the Roman road. Bear left to follow the Roman road still climbing. This narrow white lane cutting deep through the

chalk downland rising to the top of **Ridgeway Hill** has a rather eerie feel. It is said that at times of national crisis, Roman legions appear marching down to Weymouth! Thomas Hardy chose this place to begin his great epic poem *The Dynasts*.

6 At the top of the hill turn left to follow the **Ridgeway**, an old Bronze Age trading route with their circular burial mounds either side of the track. Now you have a beautiful view inland over the earth ramparts of Maiden Castle hill fort dominating the Winterborne valley, to the rooftops of Dorchester.

7 After about ½ mile you come to a sign indicating a path on the left for **Upwey** and the **Wishing Well**. Navigate carefully at this point. Do not take the obvious stony track on your left but go through a gate and turn left to go through another gate marked with a blue arrow bridleway sign.

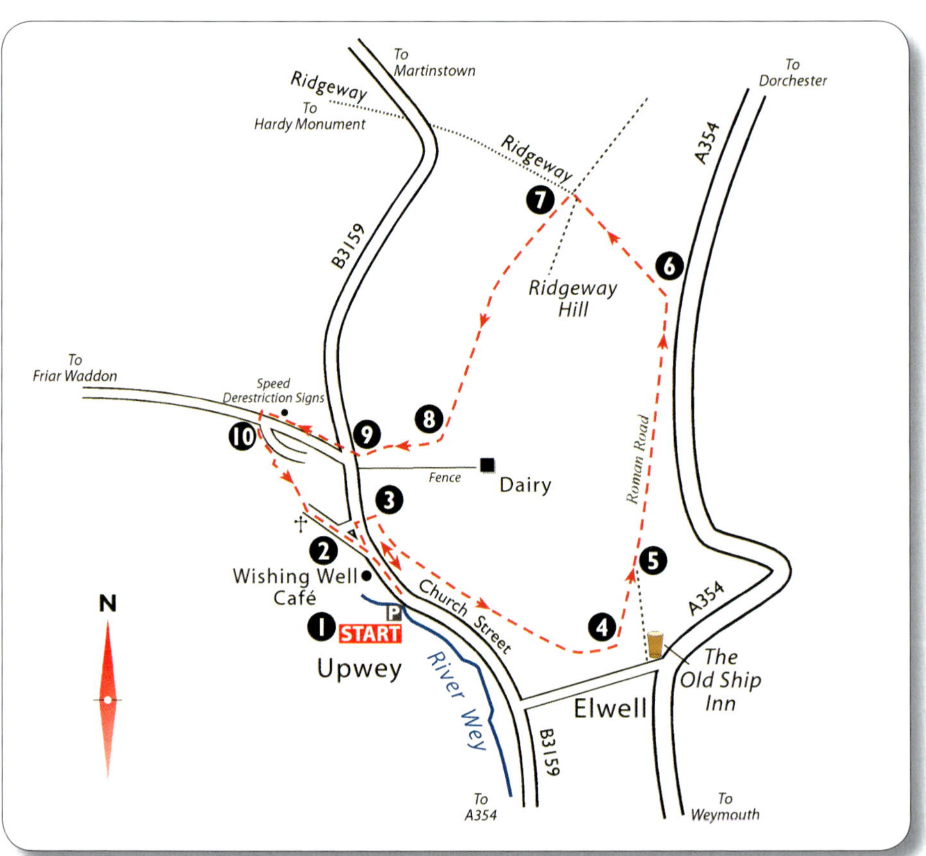

■ *The Roman road near the top of Ridgeway Hill.* ■

The path is faint but keep ahead for a few yards then bear a little right to continue down a valley passing a few small trees on your right. Go through a gate and continue along the valley.

8 There is no clear path but when you see a fence about 60 yards ahead (it leads to a track to a dairy) turn right more steeply downhill, still keeping the fence about 60 yards away on your left, to the foot of the hill. Do not go through the obvious gate on your left which leads to the track to the dairy but keep ahead through a less conspicuous gate marked with a blue arrow bridleway sign. A narrow grassy path leads you down to the B3159.

9 Cross straight over the B3159 and follow the **Friar Waddon** minor road for about 200 yards to pass speed derestriction signs. About 100 yards after the signs you come to an asphalt drive bordered by stones on your left. There is no sign but look down the drive and you will see a stile marked with a yellow arrow to the right of the drive.

10 Turn left down the drive, cross the stile on the right and follow the narrow footpath as it curves left to go over a plank bridge. The path bears left from the bridge and follows the streamside over stiles before becoming a wider track and bringing you to the road in front of **Upwey church**. Bear left along the road to return to your car.

14 Cerne Abbas

In the Haunt of a Giant

FOOTPATHS FOR FITNESS

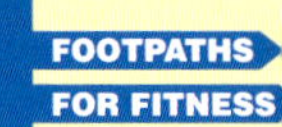

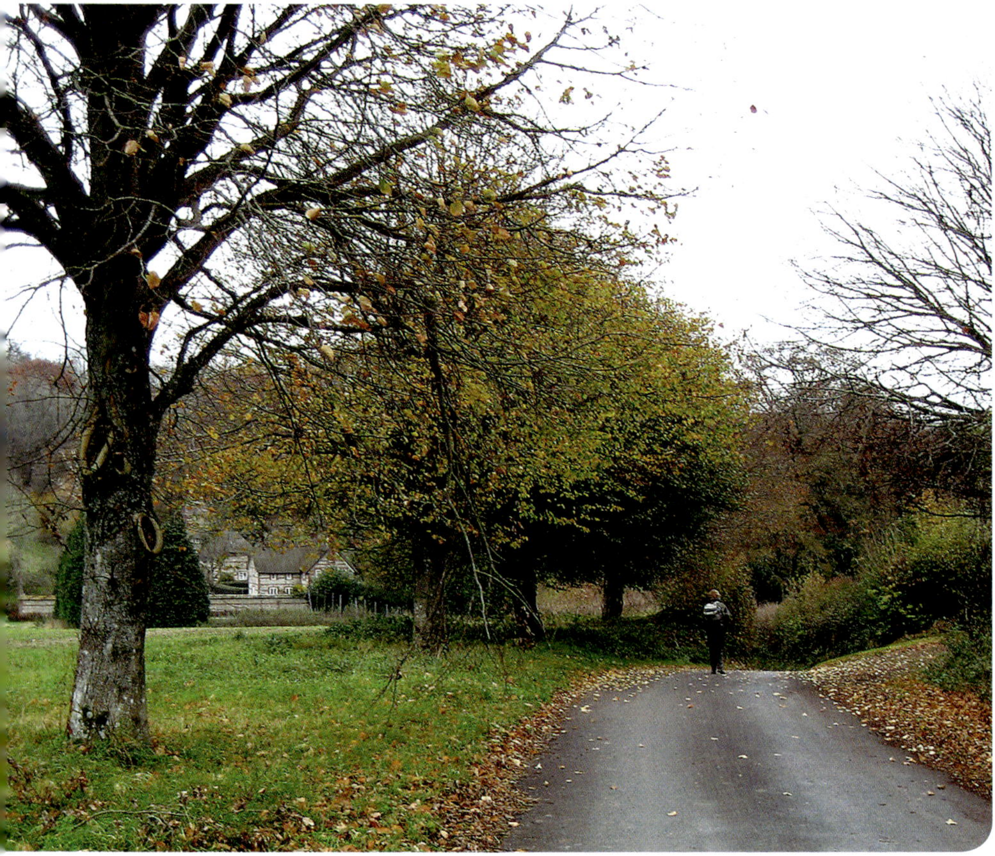

■ *Beech trees border the lane to Up Cerne.* ■

Cerne Abbas is cradled in the downs north of Dorchester. The small town grew up around a Benedictine abbey founded here in 987. Among the surviving ruins are the guesthouse and the porch to the Abbot's lodging which has a beautiful two-storey oriel window. Once an important market and manufacturing town on the main coaching routes, Cerne Abbas was bypassed by the railway and today it has become one of Dorset's most charming villages. Dominating the village on a westward-facing hillside is the famous Cerne Abbas giant, an eminently virile figure carved out of the turf, 180 ft high. It possibly dates from Romano-British times. From the village this walk takes you to Up Cerne, a tiny place with a fine manor house, then leads up high on the downs giving splendid views before returning for a short ramble round the village.

1 Turn right from the car park entrance then right again to walk up to the A352. The Giant viewing area is on your right.

2 Cross the road and turn right to walk along the grass verge beside the road, past the former workhouse on your left, for about 300 yards to a narrow lane on your left signed for **Up Cerne**.

3 Turn left to follow this pleasant lane. Through the hedge on the right you will glimpse a series of small lakes. The lane curves a little left.

4 The lane swings right to become a broad avenue bordered by beech trees at the approach to **Up Cerne**. On the right is a grey stone manor house built around 1600 and a tiny church. The lane runs downhill into a remote valley threaded by a clear chalk stream.

5 Turn left along the no-through-road to walk along the valley with the stream on your right. When the lane curves left keep straight ahead uphill.

GRADE: 2
ESTIMATED CALORIE BURN: 750

Distance: 5½ miles
Terrain: Quiet lanes and downland paths
Map: OS Explorer 117 Cerne Abbas and Bere Regis
Starting Point: Cerne Abbas car park and picnic place. GR 663015
How to get there: Cerne Abbas is about 6 miles north of Dorchester and is signed off the A352. Approaching from the south ignore the first turn on the right signed for the village and take the second lane on the right directly in front of the viewing area for the Cerne Abbas giant. Follow the sign for the picnic place for about 50 yards then turn left to the car park which is a few yards further on your left.
Refreshments: I recommend the 15th-century Royal Oak in Cerne Abbas High Street, Telephone: 01305 264382. The village also has some delightful tea shops.

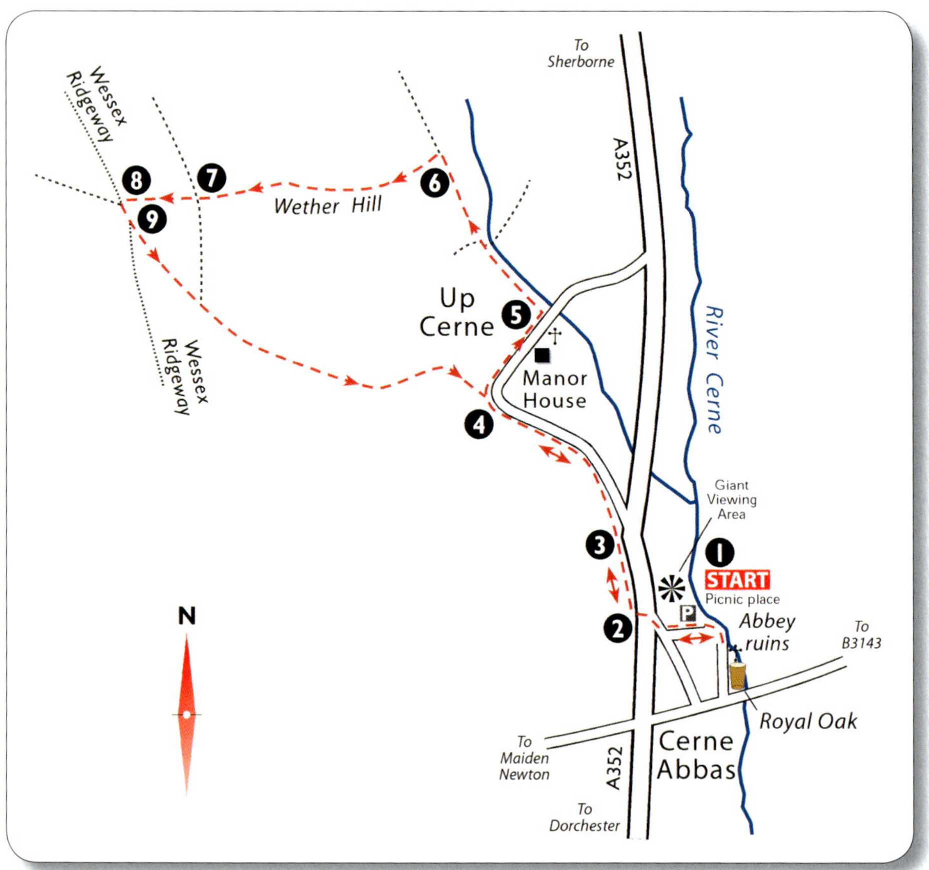

6 At the top of the hill turn left following the sign for **Wether Hill**. At first the track is hedged but it becomes a wide grassy way as it crosses the top of the down with panoramic views.

7 After almost a mile the grassy track leads up to a signpost. Our way is straight ahead following the sign for **Redpost Hill**. Navigate carefully for the next ¼ mile as there may not be a clear path at this point. If the path is not clear, walk over the field following the direction of the sign to a thick hedge on the other side. Beyond the hedge you will see a gravel track, part of the **Wessex Ridgeway** which we intend to follow. Cross the hedge to the track following a very narrow path marked by an inconspicuous post. (To find this path you may have to turn right with the hedge on your left for a short distance.)

8 Turn left along the gravel track with the hedge now on your left. On your right the hillside drops steeply into the valley of **Sydling Water**.

9 After about 300 yards the track divides by a signpost. Leave the **Ridgeway** and take the left-hand path signed for **Up Cerne**. Follow the wide grassy way ahead with a hedge on your left. Keep ahead past a track on the left. The path gradually descends over open downland then drops more steeply as it curves right to take a tree-shaded track and rejoins the outbound route at point 4. Retrace your steps down the lane to the picnic area in **Cerne Abbas**. *To explore the village* continue down the lane and turn right just before the bridge. Follow the streamside to a bridge on the left. Cross the bridge and follow the path to Abbey Street. On the right is a row of timbered and jettied houses and opposite is the mill pond and the entrance to the abbey ruins. Further down the road is Cerne Abbas church. Its treasures include some 15th-century stained glass, a Jacobean pulpit and 14th-century wall paintings. A walk down Abbey Street brings you to the High Street and the Royal Oak inn.

■ *The Cerne valley.* ■

15 Trent

Roundheads and Cavaliers

■ *Climbing the hillside from Nether Compton.* ■

Let your imagination have free play as you ramble along this walk which includes part of the Monarch's Way, a long-distance trail following the route taken by Charles II as he fled seeking sanctuary after a heavy defeat at the battle of Worcester. One of his most loyal supporters was Sir Francis Wyndham, the owner of the manor house in Trent. He hid Charles in a priest's hole in the manor and helped to plan his escape to France. Our walk begins in Trent, close to the manor. The village lies in a remote valley just west of a range of limestone hills. Little seems to have changed since Charles arrived in 1651. Many of the houses date back to the 17th century and are built of local stone varying in colour from pale gold to deep russet. From the village we follow the Trent Brook to Nether Compton, another golden stone village. A short climb is rewarded by stunning views before we return to Trent through the meadows of a beautiful valley following Charles for almost 2 miles along the Monarch's Way.

GRADE: 2
ESTIMATED CALORIE BURN: 700

Distance: 4½ miles
Terrain: Easy walking, some gentle climbing
Map: OS Explorer 129 Yeovil and Sherborne (East and West sheets)
Starting Point: Trent church GR 590185
How to get there: Trent is in north-west Dorset, close to the border with Somerset, 2 miles north of the A30 between Yeovil and Sherborne. Turn off the A30 following the sign for Over Compton. At the crossroads keep ahead signed Trent and after about a mile turn right for the village. Pass Trent church and Chantry House on the left, then turn immediately left to park on the left by the wall at the approach to the churchyard.
Refreshments: The Rose and Crown, an old-world thatched pub, friendly, with excellent food and drink. Telephone: 01935 850776.

1 Cross the churchyard to visit **Trent church**. Among much of interest you will see a magnificent 15th-century rood screen, pre-Reformation pews and a finely carved Dutch pulpit dating from around 1600. In the porch an old notice sternly requests that 'All persons … take off pattens and clogs before entering'. As you return to the road you pass the **Chantry House** on your right, now a private dwelling. It was built around 1400 and was originally the home of the chantry priest. There are glimpses of the manor from the north side of the churchyard. Turn right along the road towards the sign for the **Rose and Crown**, then turn left following the footpath sign for **Nether Compton** passing the pub car park on your right. The path continues past the pub entrance to a gate.

2 Through the gate follow the footpath straight ahead across the field. (If you look back the path is directly in line with the spire of the church.) Go over a wooden footbridge to a lane.

3 Turn right. The lane drops downhill towards the **Trent Brook**.

4 Before the brook, turn left along a thickly hedged cobbled bridleway and follow it for almost a mile with the brook on your right to a road in **Nether Compton**. Bear right to the **Griffin's Head pub**. Turn right, following the sign for **Sherborne**, to walk through the village which is grouped around a large village green. I was told that sheep races are held each year on

the green, the sheep being helped on their way to the winning post by the shepherdess with a large bucket of nuts! Just past the green is the beautifully cared for church of **St Nicholas**. One of the church's most attractive features is the late 15th-century stone rood screen. The millennium has been commemorated with a plaque let into the floor. Continue along the pavement which stops just before the village hall on the left.

4 Navigate carefully at this point. Pass the village hall. Do not turn left immediately in front of the building but turn left a few feet beyond it with a wall on your left and garages on your right. This looks unlikely but a grassy path leads up the bank ahead and now a clear path climbs gently beside the meadows with a hedge on the left. As you gain height you will enjoy magnificent views west over Somerset. Trent, distinguished by its church spire – one of very few in Dorset – lies half hidden by trees in its remote valley.

6 Go through a gate and turn left along a sunken cobbled track. Keep to the track for almost 1 mile as it weaves its way gently uphill past a path on the left and swings right to a crossing track with a large barn on the right.

7 Turn left along the grassy path to a T-junction.

The village green in Nether Compton.

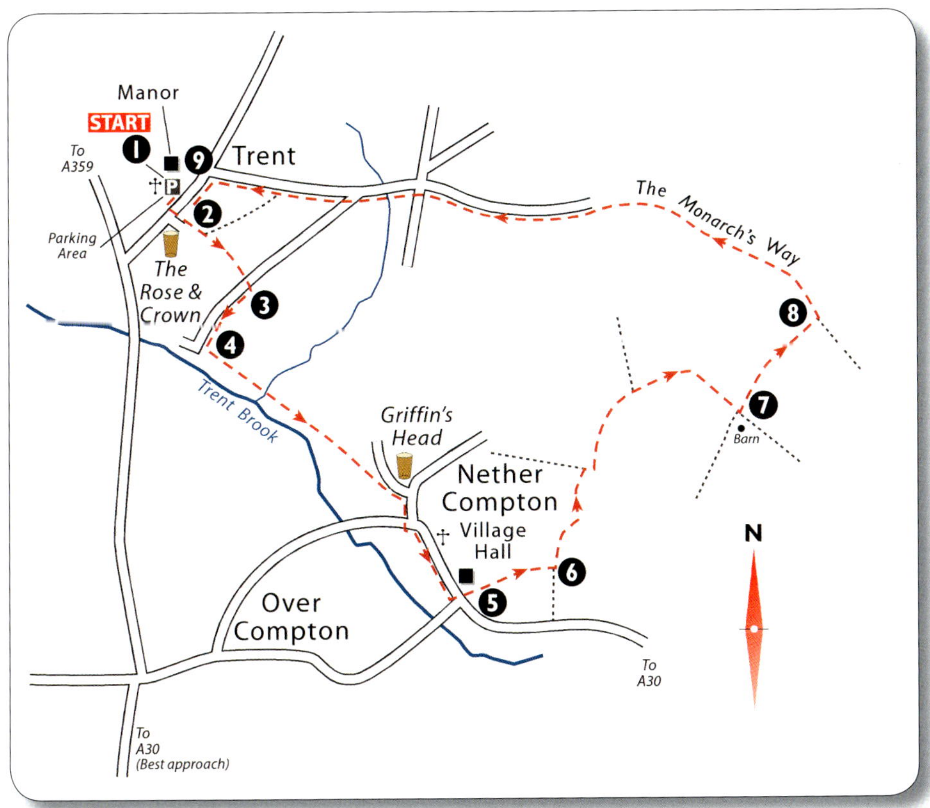

8 Turn left to follow the **Monarch's Way** downhill through the trees. Continue past a gate to a small wooden gate which opens to flower-filled meadows sloping steeply downhill. The path leads down to a gate. Go through, and bear right along a hedged track which brings you to a road in **Trent** passing a small pond on the right. Keep straight on over a lane to walk through the village to a T-junction.

9 Turn left signed for **Over Compton** and **Yeovil** to return to the church and your car.

The route of the Monarch's Way, which is 615 miles long, was devised by Trevor Antill. He describes the way-marked route in detail in three volumes published by Meridian Books. Each one is divided into sections enabling you to plan suitable day-walks. There is a Monarch's Way Association. Telephone 0121 429 4397.

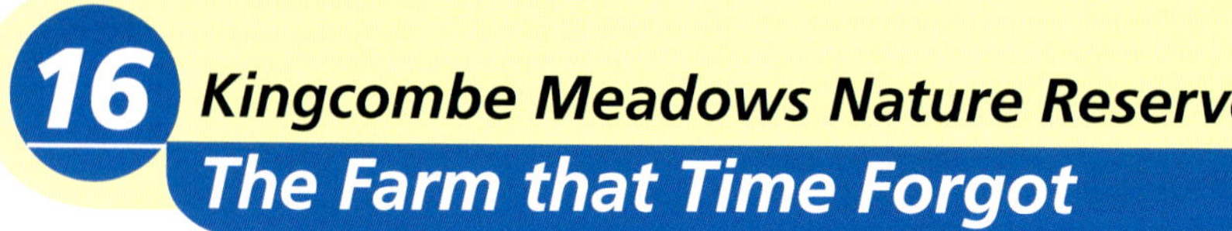

16 Kingcombe Meadows Nature Reserve

The Farm that Time Forgot

FOOTPATHS FOR FITNESS

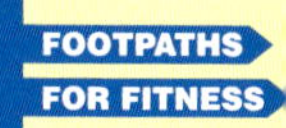

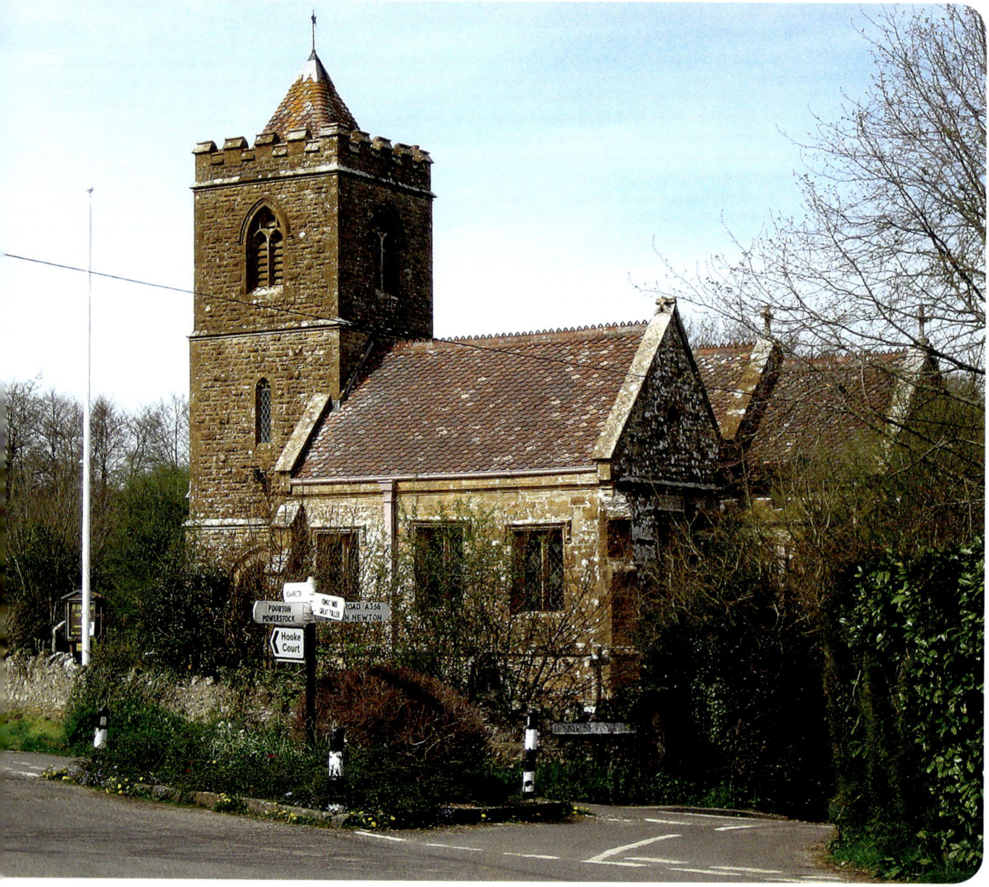

■ *Hooke church.* ■

If you would like to walk in a corner of Dorset that has seen few changes since the days of Thomas Hardy then come to Kingcombe Meadows, a reserve of national importance run by the Dorset Wildlife Trust. The land around the hamlet of Lower Kingcombe in the valley of the river Hooke has always been farmed according to traditional methods without the use of herbicides, pesticides and artificial fertilisers and the trust carries on this tradition today. The result is a landscape of great beauty – a patchwork of small thickly hedged fields, hay meadows full of wild flowers in June attracting hordes of butterflies, and wet rush-filled pastures. The whole area is interlaced with narrow lanes and gently flowing streams. Our walk starts close to the Kingcombe Centre, which has direct access to the reserve. We walk through the meadows to Hooke, a tiny riverside village, then climb the down to enjoy views over the Hooke valley. We stroll through Kingcombe Wood – famous for its bluebells – before returning along sunken tracks bordered by coppiced hazels.

1 Turn left from the car park entrance and follow **Kingcombe Road** for about 100 yards. When the road swings left keep straight on along **Mount Pleasant Lane**, an attractive tree-shaded track.

2 Do not go through the gate to continue along the lane but bear right and go through the gate into **Coarse Mead**. Bear left to walk over the meadows of the reserve. We came this way in late April and the ground was golden with primroses. At the top of a rise, shaded by a mighty oak, stands a Purbeck stone erected in memory of Richard Jennings. It is inscribed 'He loved no less his fellow man but loved he nature more'.

GRADE: 2
ESTIMATED CALORIE BURN: 500

Distance: 4½ miles
Terrain: Meadow and woodland paths. Some paths could be wet. One fairly steep but short climb.
Map: OS Explorer 117 Cerne Abbas and Bere Regis
Starting point: Dorset Wildlife Trust's main car park at Pound Cottage in Lower Kingcombe. GR 554990
How to get there: The reserve is about 13 miles west of Dorchester. Turn off the A356 for Toller Porcorum. Turn right in Toller Porcorum for Lower Kingcombe, about a mile along the valley. At the time of writing the entrance to the car park was not marked. If this is still the case look carefully for a narrow stony track on the right with signs for the Dorset Wildlife Trust on either side. Turn right for a few yards up the track to the car park. The Kingcombe Centre is a little further down the road also on the right.
Refreshments: None at the time of writing but they will be available when the new Wildlife Trust Visitor Centre is completed.

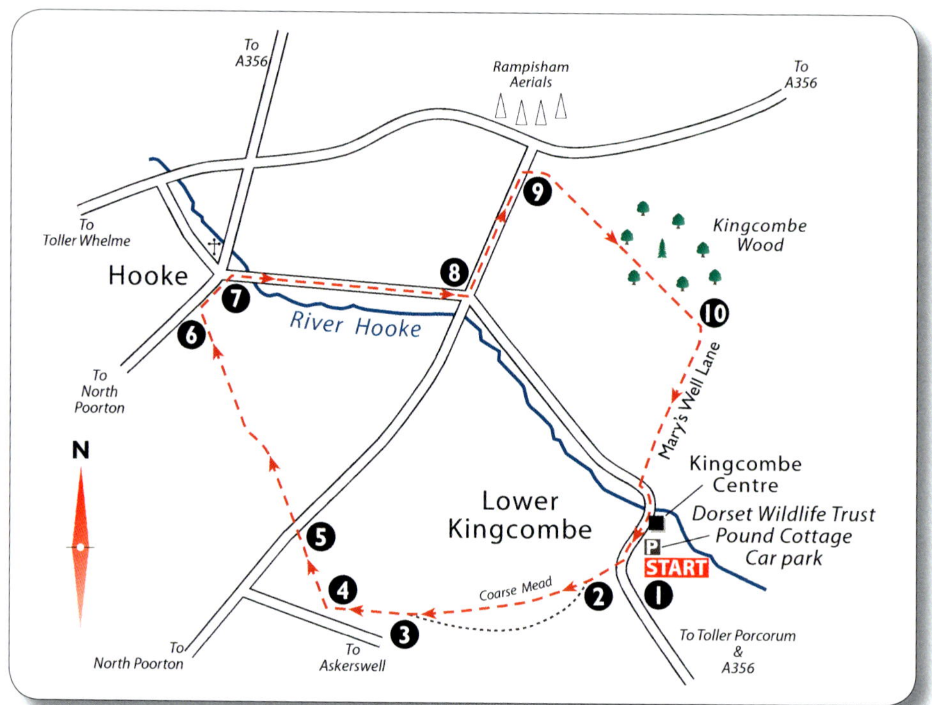

3 At this point the meadow path rejoins the continuation of the lane. The path rises giving wide views over the **Hooke valley**. Go through a gap in a hedge to walk along a grassy ridge. After going through another gap the path descends to lead through a gate. Keep straight on a little uphill with a hedge a few yards away on your left. Continue through another gate with the hedge now closer on your left to a gate on your left before a lane.

4 Do not go through the gate to the lane but turn right with a hedge close on your left. Go through a gate and continue beside the hedge to go through another gate to a lane.

5 Cross the lane and follow the track ahead. Keep straight on through a gate towards the rooftops of **Hooke village**. The track drops downhill through a wood and leads to a gate opening to a lane.

6 Turn right and follow the lane to a T-junction in front of **Hooke church** which dates from the 15th century and is built of local red limestone.

7 Turn right through the village to cross a bridge over the **river Hooke** and follow the quiet road for about ¾ mile to a crossroads.

8 Turn left uphill following the sign for **Rampisham**. You will see the aerials on top of the hill ahead. Before it reaches the aerials the lane leads downhill into a valley.

9 Turn right to walk along the valley floor following the sign for **Lower Kingcombe**. Continue through a gate to go through a small gate marked with the blue arrow bridleway sign leading into **Kingcombe Wood**. The scent of the bluebells as we walked through the wood was almost overpowering!

10 Leave the wood through another waymarked gate and keep straight on over the meadow. The next gate opens to a well-defined track sunk deep between banks crowned with ancient hedges. This is **Mary's Well Lane** and brings you to **Lower Kingcombe Road**. Turn left along the road which curves right past the **Kingcombe Centre** to bring you back to your car.

■ *Kingcombe Wood, carpeted with bluebells in May.* ■

17 Golden Cap & Langdon Wood

The Dorset Coast at Your Feet

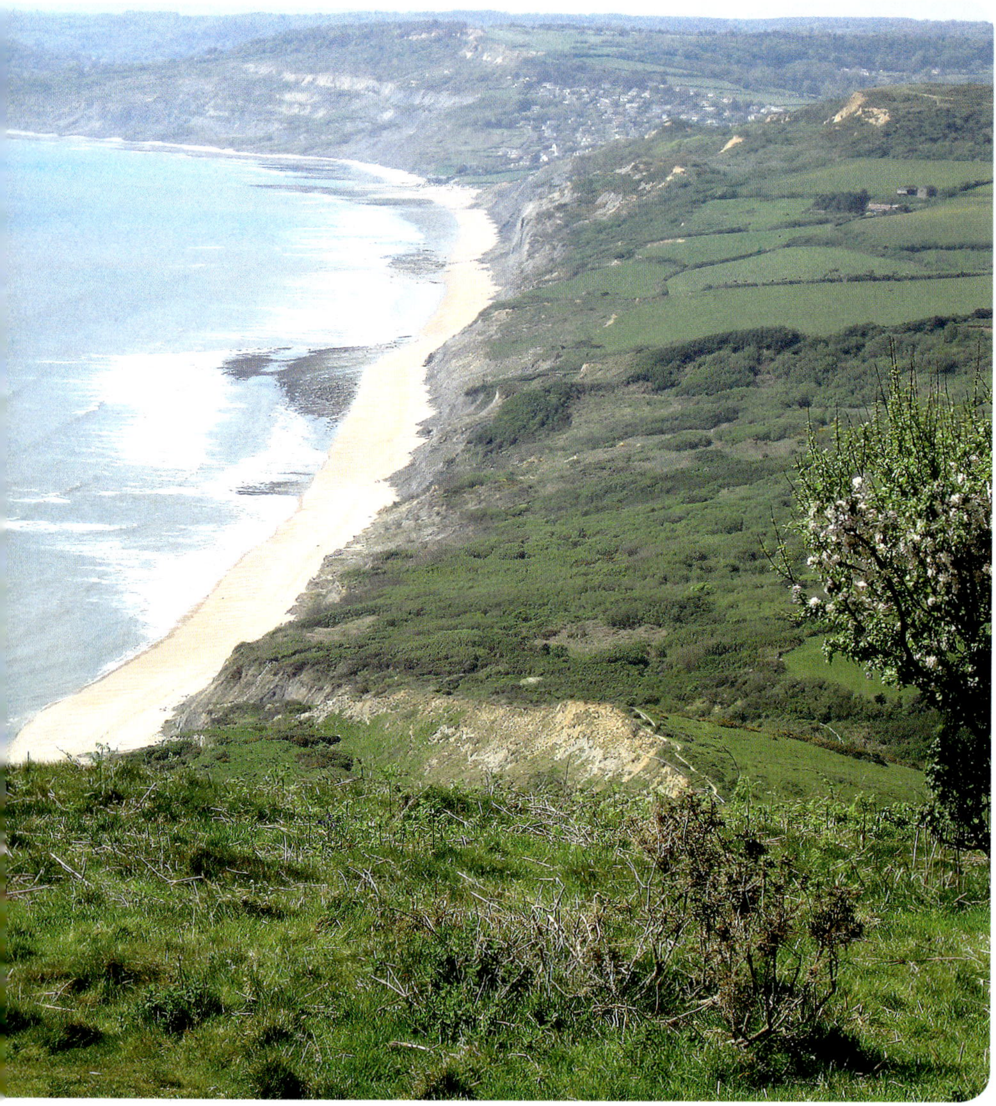

■ *Looking east from Golden Cap.* ■

GRADE: 2
ESTIMATED CALORIE BURN: 350

Distance: 3½ miles
Terrain: Although this is not a long walk, some climbing is involved
Map: OS Explorer 116 Lyme Regis and Bridport
Starting Point: Langdon Wood National Trust car park (sometimes signed Golden Cap car park.) GR 413931
How to get there: Langdon Wood car park is not easy to find but the walk is well worth the effort! Approach from the east along the A35. Drive through Chideock and continue uphill for about ½ mile. Just before the dual carriageway turn left down a narrow unsigned road. It is the first turning on the left after leaving Chideock. After about 40 yards turn left again in front of a no-through-road sign along a track signed Golden Cap car park. About 300 yards further on you will see a large notice for Langdon Wood car park (alias Golden Cap car park) on the right. Turn right to drive up to the car park.
Refreshments: None on the route but I suggest the Anchor pub in nearby Seatown. Telephone: 01297 489215.

Golden Cap is the highest cliff on the south coast soaring sheer from the sea to a height of 618 ft. It is crowned by an exposed layer of Upper Greensand which shines bright orange in the sun. From the top on a clear day you can enjoy views west over the great arc of Lyme Bay as far as Start Point in Devon, east to Portland, and inland over the Marshwood Vale to some of the county's loftiest hills including Pilsdon Pen and Lewesdon. The whole area around Golden Cap is owned by the National Trust and is rich in wildlife. Your walk to the Cap starts with a stroll along a terraced path through Langdon Wood carpeted with bluebells and scented with wild garlic in early summer. You leave the wood to cross the open hillside below the summit of Golden Cap before climbing the steps to the top. A path through a different part of the wood leads you back to your car.

1 From the car park follow the sign for **Golden Cap** past a gate. A broad track leads you along the hillside through mature beech and oak trees, beside the eastern fringe of **Langdon Wood**. **Chideock** lies in the valley on your left. The track curves right round the southern edge of the wood to a division.

2 Take the left-hand path and descend to a signpost. Turn left following the

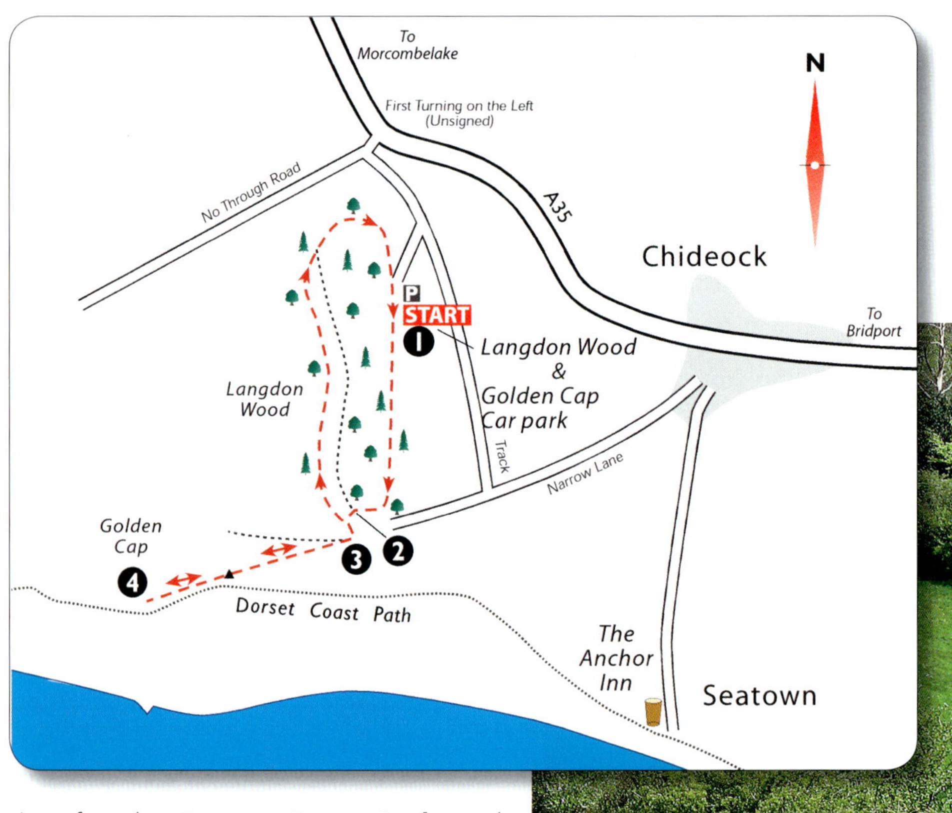

sign for the **Dorset Coast Path** and **Golden Cap** and walk downhill past a barrier.

3 Turn right still following the sign for the Dorset Coast Path and Golden Cap past a gate. **Golden Cap** is directly ahead. Take the left of two grassy paths to climb the hillside. Cross the squeeze stile following the signs for **Golden Cap** and climb the steps to the flat summit of the cliff marked with a trig point. Your reward for the climb is the spectacular view! To see more fine views inland and a little further over **Lyme Bay** bear right along the summit to its most easterly point.

4 Retrace your steps downhill to the gate. Turn left uphill following the sign for **Langdon Wood**. Before you come to your outbound track turn left again following another sign for the wood. Follow the grassy footpath along the wood's western edge. Beech trees shade your path on the right and on the left runs a thick overgrown coppice hedge, a haven for wildlife. The path curves a little uphill to meet a crosstrack. Bear left around the northern fringe of the wood to return to the car park.

■ *The return route to Langdon Wood.* ■

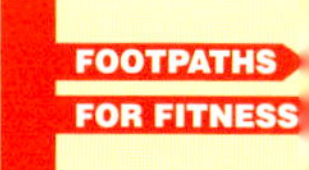

18 Gussage All Saints & Harley Down

Drovers' Tracks and a Roman Road

FOOTPATHS FOR FITNESS

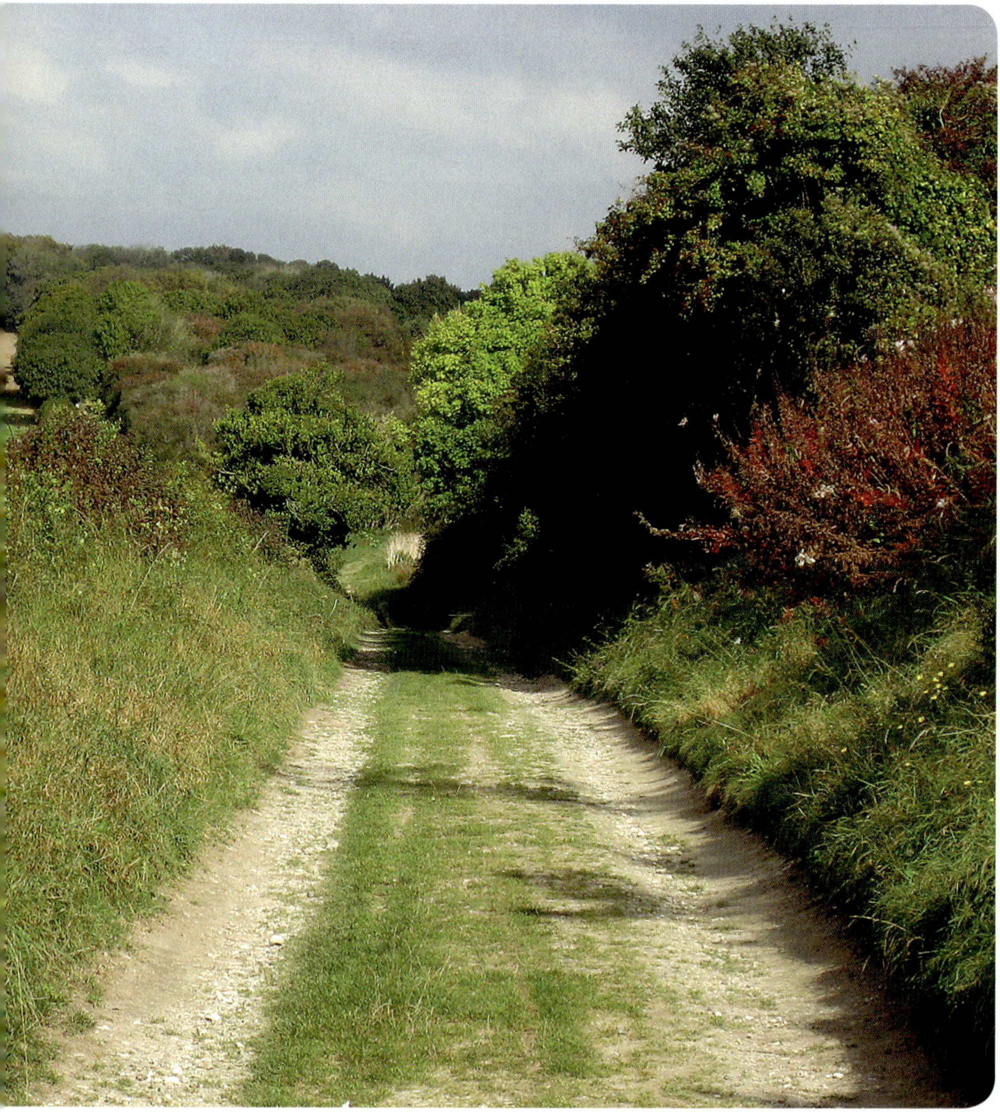

A drover's road near Gussage All Saints.

Gussage All Saints is a remote village situated among the uplands of Cranborne Chase. A clear chalk stream overhung with willows runs past the village under a series of small bridges. No scene could be more peaceful but in the past these quiet downs must have looked very different, as you will discover as you follow the route of this walk. From the village we follow drovers' tracks past Harley Wood to the top of Gussage Down crossed by Ackling Dyke, a road constructed by the Romans in the 1st century AD to link Old Sarum just north of Salisbury (little of Old Sarum remains) and Durnovaria, today's Dorchester. A ridge path heading westward leads us past the banks and ditches of a large Celtic settlement. Reminders of an earlier people, the first farmers, are two well preserved Neolithic Long Barrows. One of these large communal tombs is carefully aligned with the Dorset Cursus, a six-mile-long parallel pair of banks and ditches which was possibly used for ceremonial purposes. You will see a remnant of its southerly embankment beside the path. As you return to the village the path leads beneath magnificent beech trees, the pride of Cranborne Chase.

1 Walk up **Harley Lane** passing the church on your left and **College Farm** on your right. The track rises gently between high banks then levels to follow the side of a shallow valley. After about 1 mile the track descends past turnings to the left and right.

GRADE: 3
ESTIMATED CALORIE BURN: 800

Distance: 6½ miles
Terrain: Grassy tracks, some climbing
Map: OS Explorer 118 Shaftesbury and Cranborne Chase
Starting Point: Parking area beside Harley Lane in Gussage All Saints. GR 999108
How to get there: Gussage All Saints is about 7 miles east of Blandford Forum. Turn for the village off the A354 Blandford Forum – Salisbury road. Drive through Gussage St Michael. Bear left over the bridge into Gussage All Saints. Do not follow the road as it curves right but keep straight ahead passing the cross on your right into Harley Lane. There is room to park beside the churchyard wall on your left.
Refreshments: The Drover's Inn, Gussage All Saints. Telephone: 01258 840084.

2 Keep straight ahead with the trees of **Harley Wood** on your left and a fence bordering fields on your right. When the gravelled track you are following curves right continue along the grassy path ahead. The path runs close to the edge of coppiced woodland.

3 The path runs deeper into the tangled woods of **Dancing Drove** and brings you to a crossway. Bear right along the path which runs close to the edge of the wood curving north to a junction marked with the green arrows of the **Jubilee Trail**.

4 Turn left to walk the few yards to meet **Ackling Dyke** at **Harley Gap**. Cross the Roman road, climb the embankment and follow the track ahead heading west along the top of **Gussage Down**. The view northwards over Wiltshire is superb. After about ½ mile look for the remains of the Celtic settlement beside the track on your right. When the track curves right keep straight ahead along the grassy path following the ridge to pass a Long Barrow on your left.

5 As you approach another Long Barrow on the left you cross a low ridge, a remnant of the **Dorset Cursus**. The Cursus originally enclosed 220 acres and the labour and tribal organisation involved in constructing it must have been immense. These now-lonely downs must once have been well populated. Retrace your steps to cross **Ackling Dyke** and return to point 4 at **Harley Gap**. Keep straight ahead following the **Jubilee Trail** heading east along the top of **Harley Down**.

6 After about a mile the track leaves the **Jubilee Trail** and curves right for about 100 yards. Then it swings left to continue eastwards beside a wood.

7 After about ¼ mile the track curves left. At the corner turn right with a hedge on your left – purple with sloes in autumn – and a wood on your right. When you come to an open field bear right beside the field with trees on your right. The path swings right through the trees to a crosstrack.

■ *Gussage All Saints seen across the meadows.* ■

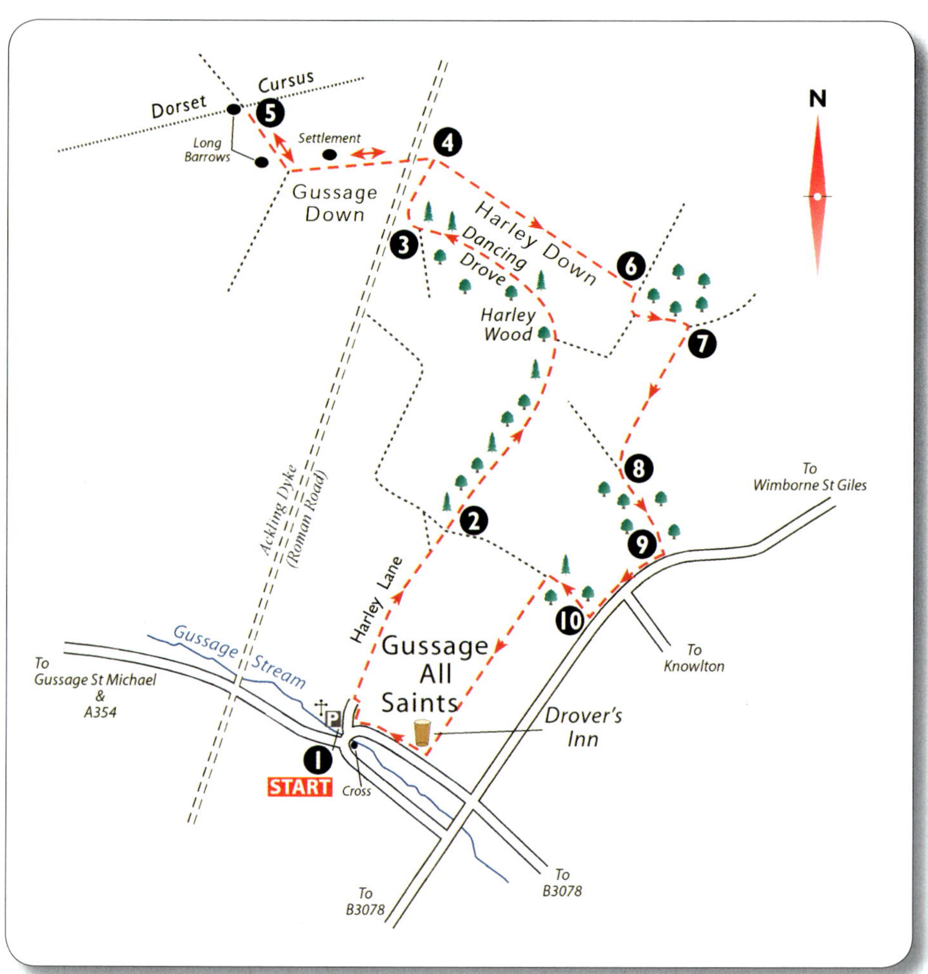

8 Turn left to follow a path bordered by beech trees to a lane.

9 Turn right down the lane past the turning for **Knowlton**. Walk up the rise ahead and at the top take the bridleway on the right through a gate.

10 Continue for about ¼ mile then take the first track on the left which drops gently downhill to the road in **Gussage All Saints** beside the **Drover's Inn**. Turn right and walk through the village to return to your car.

19 Houns-Tout & Chapman's Pool

The Jurassic Coast

■ *Descending the valley above Chapman's Pool.* ■

This superb walk follows a ridge in the Purbeck Hills to the sea. We start from Kingston, a small hilltop village built and roofed with locally-quarried dove-grey limestone. Cottages and gardens blend naturally with their surroundings and little seems to have changed since Thomas Hardy walked its quiet lanes, gathering inspiration for his novel, *The Hand of Ethelberta*. We follow him to the sea along the crest of a valley known locally as the Golden Bowl. The hillsides drop smooth and sheer to the wooded banks of a stream and at the seaward end you will see Encombe House, an 18th-century mansion which Hardy called 'Enkworth House'. From the headland at Houns-tout, the views are breathtaking. Portland lies to the west and near at hand a jagged range of cliffs rises to St Aldhelm's Head. As we head east along the coast path our way runs above Chapman's Pool, an incredibly blue, scallop-shaped bay. Then a complete change of scene as we return along the Purbeck Way following a wooded valley and crossing the fields to Kingston. From the fields a view of Corfe Castle gives the perfect finishing touch to this unmissable walk.

1 The track to **Houns-tout** runs just beyond the car park. Take the narrow path through the trees from the far end of the car park to join the Houns-tout track and turn right. When you meet a crossing track bear left past a private track on the left and keep ahead to a Y-junction. Bear left a little uphill. The track runs through the **Kingston Plantation**.

GRADE: 3
ESTIMATED CALORIE BURN: 850

Distance: 6½ miles
Terrain: Coastal paths, rocky in places. One steep descent down steps, care needed.
Map: OS Outdoor Leisure 15 Purbeck and South Dorset
Starting Point: Car park in woods west of Kingston village. GR 953795
How to get there: Head south from Wareham along the A351. Drive through Corfe Castle then bear right along the B3069 for Kingston. At the top of the hill in the village leave the B3069 and turn right passing the front of the Scott Arms on your right. Keep straight on passing the church on your left signed for Encombe. Continue past the private drive to Kingston House and the start of the footpath to Houns-tout. Keep straight on for about 50 yards to the car park among the trees on your left.
Refreshments: The Scott Arms, Kingston. Telephone: 01929 480270.

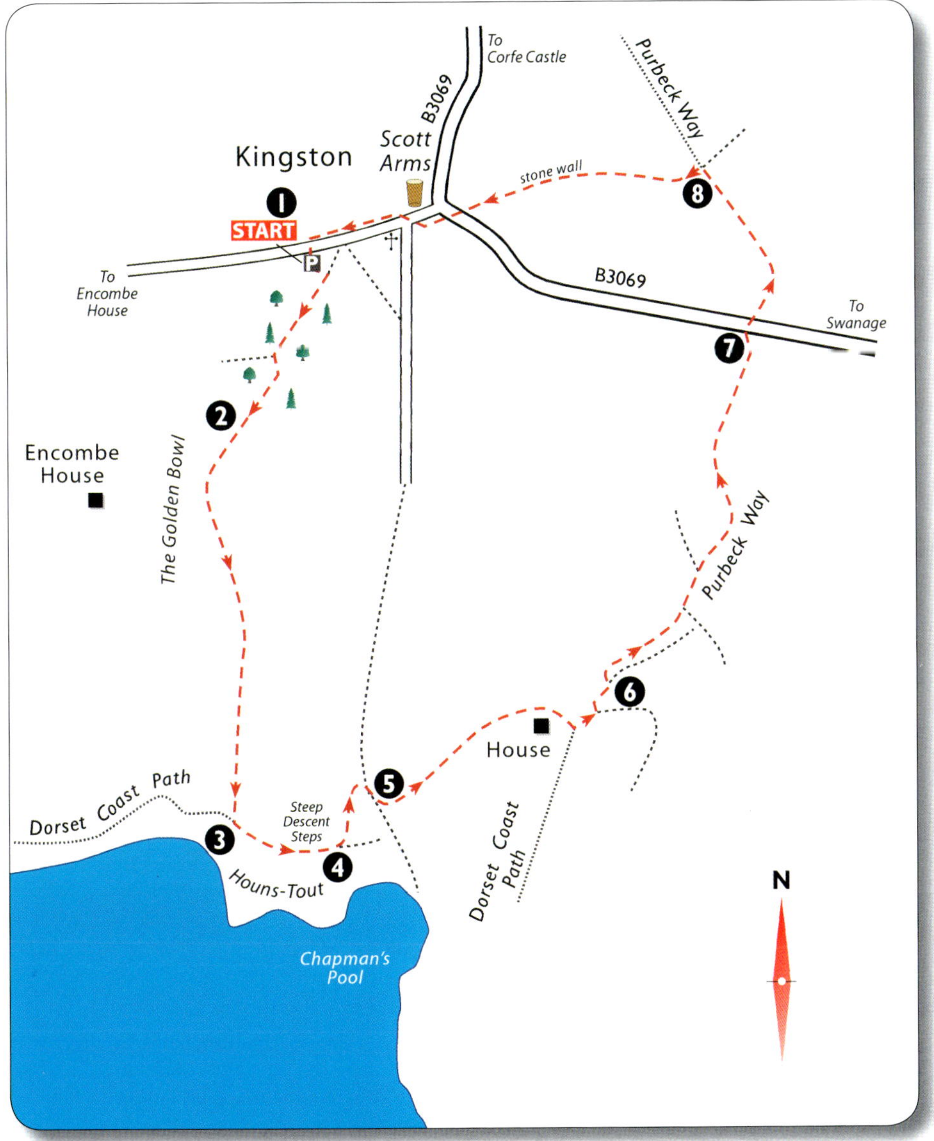

2 Cross a stile and the trees give way to open downland and the view over the **Golden Bowl**. Follow the path over stiles along the crest of the hill for about 2 miles to meet the coast path as it rises to the clifftop at **Houns-tout**. A thoughtfully-placed stone seat makes an ideal place to stop and enjoy the views.

3 Continue along the clifftop path round the headland. As the path curves left you will see the clear-cut outline of **Chapman's Pool** fringed by dark sinister-looking cliffs. Descend the steep flight of steps with care to a stile at the foot of the hill.

4 The coast path is diverted inland at this point. So turn left over the stile. Keep straight on over the meadow with the hillside at first close on your left. The path swings right to a stile by a gate. Cross the stile and continue over a causeway to a white concrete track. Turn right for a few yards then leave the concrete track and turn left along a grassy path with a fence on the right.

5 Follow the path as it runs through a valley. Cross a stile and walk past the side of a house to a lane. Turn right and follow the lane as it crosses the stream in the valley. Here we leave the coast path and keep to the lane as it curves left signed for the **Purbeck Way**. Follow the lane for about 150 yards.

6 You come to a signpost indicating a left turn up the hill for **Kingston**. Surprising as this appears this is the **Purbeck Way**! So turn left and after a few yards the path bears right to wind gently up another lovely valley. Keep ahead past a stile on your right and a joining track on the left to go through a gate. The path curves left to rise more steeply then curves right through a gate. Continue to the top of the hill then follow the path with a fence on your right. Go through a gap on your left and follow the hedged path through a gate to a post. Bear left to the B3069.

7 Cross the road and take the track signed for **Corfe Castle**. Continue downhill through gates for about ½ mile and look for a post on your left marked with footpath signs.

8 Turn left along a narrow path through bushes and cross a stile to emerge on the open hillside with a stone wall on your right. Keep the wall on your right to walk along the hillside through gates and follow the wall as it curves left uphill. Cross a stile to meet the B3069 in **Kingston**. Turn right to walk through the village passing the **Scott Arms** on your right to return to your car.

■ *The Golden Bowl and Encombe House.* ■

20 Burton Bradstock

A River Valley in the Western Hills

Crossing the river Bride.

This walk links two villages, Burton Bradstock beside the river Bride, and Shipton Gorge high on a hilltop to the north. The route starts beside Burton Beach (also known as Hive Beach) so you have an opportunity to burn off a few more calories with a swim! From the beach we cross the meadows to Burton Bradstock village. The 15th-century church is surrounded by a maze of narrow lanes winding between cottages built of pale gold stone. After a ramble beside the Bride we follow the course of a tributary stream up the valley towards Shipton Gorge's hilltop church. There is no gorge here – the village belonged to the de Gorge family in the 13th century – just an attractive cluster of houses and cottages with gardens that spill colour into the road. We return to Burton Bradstock over the top of North Hill with views far inland to Pilsdon Pen and Lewesdon Hill. A short ramble along the coast path brings you back to your car.

GRADE: 3
ESTIMATED CALORIE BURN: 850

Distance: 6 miles
Terrain: Meadow paths and lanes. Some gradual climbs, one steep but short climb up North Hill.
Map: OS Outdoor Leisure 15 Purbeck and South Dorset
Starting Point: Hive Beach (Burton Beach) car park. GR 491889
How to get there: Approach via the B3157 and follow the signs for Hive Beach car park down Beach Road.
Refreshments: Hive Beach café is by the car park. Telephone. 01308 897070. I recommend the Three Horseshoes pub in Burton Bradstock in the High Street. Telephone 01308 897259.

1 Walk back up **Beach Road** to the B3157. Turn left for about 150 yards and look carefully for a signpost marked 'Village ¼ ' to the right of the road.

2 Cross the road and follow the footpath over two stone stiles to a lane. Over the lane, go through a gate and keep straight ahead over a meadow to cross a small footbridge over the **Bride**. A streamside path brings you to a road. Follow this to the church on your left.

3 Opposite the church turn right along **Darby Lane** and at the end of the lane turn right along **Grove Road** leading to the riverside. On the left you will see 18th-century **Grove House**, once the home of Richard Roberts, an enterprising mill owner. Before the trade moved to Bridport, Burton Bradstock had three mills processing locally-grown flax and hemp, and manufacturing linens and sailcloth. A little further down the lane you will see a flax-swingling mill, (now flats) complete with some of its workings. To swingle flax was to dress it by breaking down the non-fibrous parts of the flax stems. The soft stems could then be drawn into long strands to make linen.

4 Beyond the mill, keep straight ahead along the footpath beside the **river Bride**. When the footpath meets a track, turn left for a few yards to meet **Annings Lane**.

5 Bear right and follow the lane for about ¾ mile past a bridleway sign on the left to a footpath sign on the left.

6 Turn left as indicated along a track, passing a bungalow on your right. Go through a gate and follow the path up the valley with a stream on your right. Shortly after passing a field gate in a dip on your right, the path curves a little downhill to the stream.

7 Cross the stepping stones over the stream, go through a gate and turn left towards **Cathole Copse**. Continue up the valley through gates keeping the wood on your right.

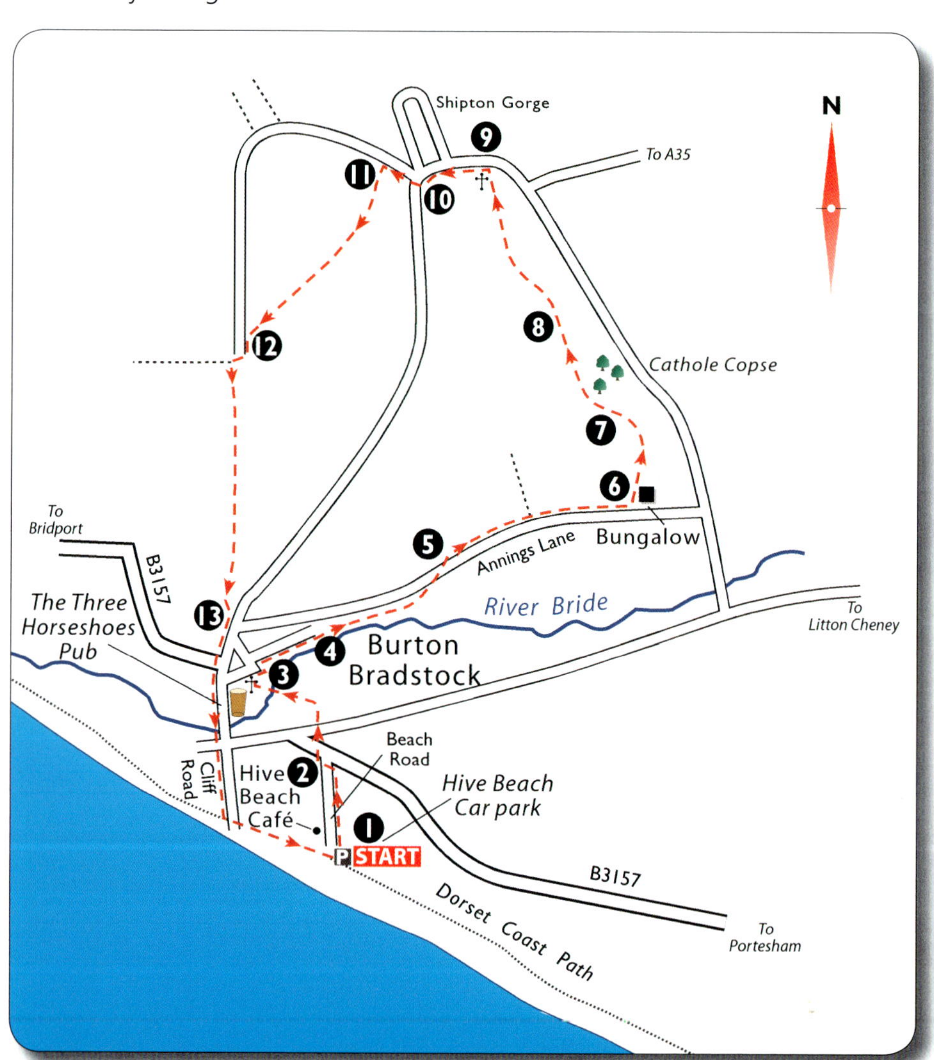

8 The path drops to a stile on your right. Over the stile bear left, cross a small bridge over a stream and keep ahead over meadows and stiles to climb the hillside to a wooden gate to the right of **Shipton Gorge church**. Walk down the hill to the village.

9 Turn left through the village and keep straight ahead following the sign for **Burton Bradstock**, passing a small red pillar box on your left to a T-junction.

10 Cross the road and follow the track ahead to a footpath sign on the left.

11 Turn left into the meadows. We found no clear path at this point, but keep ahead over two meadows and stiles. Now bear slightly right following the

■ *Shipton Gorge.* ■

direction of the yellow arrow footpath signs over the next three meadows and an assortment of stiles to an iron farm gate beside a footpath fingerpost.

12 Turn left up a track to a cross-track. Bear right for a few yards then take the bridleway on the left leading downhill. Climb **North Hill** keeping a hedge on your left then follow the field path downhill to go through a gate to a track which brings you to a road in **Burton Bradstock**. Turn right and follow the road as it curves right to the **High Street**.

13 Turn left through the village and when the main road curves left keep straight on up **Cliff Road** to the coast path along the cliff top. Turn left along the coast path to return to **Hive Beach**.

Calorie Chart

The following chart shows the approximate calories spent per hour by a person weighing 8 stone (112 lbs), 11 stone (154 lbs) and 15 stone (210 lbs)

	8 stone	**11 stone**	**15 stone**
Walking, 2 mph	160	240	312
Walking, 3 mph	210	320	416
Walking, 4½ mph	295	440	572

Note that these figures are based on moderate, not vigorous, activity.